A Light
Unto My Path

A Light
Unto My Path

CRAFTING EFFECTIVE HOMILIES

James J. Bacik

AND

Kevin E. Anderson

Paulist Press
New York/Mahwah, N.J.

Cover design by Sharyn Banks
Book design by Lynn Else
Cover photo by Anton de Flon

Library of Congress Cataloging-in-Publication Data

Bacik, James J., 1936–
A light unto my path : crafting effective homilies / James J. Bacik and Kevin E. Anderson.
   p. cm.
   Includes bibliographical references.
   ISBN 0-8091-4376-3 (alk. paper)
   1. Catholic Church—Sermons. 2. Lectionary preaching—Catholic Church.
I. Anderson, Kevin E. II. Title.
BX1756.A1B33 2006
251—dc22

                                    2005023196

Published by Paulist Press
997 Macarthur Boulevard
Mahwah, New Jersey 07430

www.paulistpress.com

Printed and bound in the
United States of America

Contents

DEDICATION

We dedicate this book to Richard McCormick, SJ (1922–2000), the outstanding moral theologian who taught both of us that Christian teaching does indeed illumine the path leading to the Gracious Mystery.

Introduction

This book is the product of a long-standing dialogue between myself—James Bacik, a pastor and a theologian—and Kevin Anderson, a clinical psychologist, author of two books and columnist for many Catholic newspapers around the country. About twenty years ago Kevin spent a year as a ministry assistant at Corpus Christi University Parish, where I have served as pastor for over two decades. Along with the rest of our staff, we met weekly to pray together and help prepare the homily for the following weekend. After Kevin completed his doctorate in psychology at Ohio State University, he set up practice in Toledo, and our dialogue on preaching continued, sustained by our shared desire to help homilists do a better job. After examining the literature on homiletics, we decided that there was a need for more data on preaching effectiveness, and so with my assistance Kevin designed a survey that we distributed locally and randomly around the country in 1994. The data we collected proved to be quite valuable, and we have incorporated the information into our workshops on preaching. More recently, we repeated a shortened version of the survey on a local level and have included the new material in this volume.

In writing this book, we decided to continue the dialogic approach that has worked well for us in the past. I wrote this introduction and the following chapters from my perspective as a pastor who preaches weekly and a theologian heavily influenced by the German Jesuit Karl Rahner but happy to draw as well on the thought of other influential scholars. Kevin read this material and added his responses to the text, drawing on our research data and his distinctive slant as a psychologist and regular hearer of the preached Word. In each chapter, I continued the conversation by responding to his comments. We think this dialogue between a pastor and a psychologist, enriched by our survey material, gives this book a distinctive place in the vast literature on preaching.

We have written the book for all men and women who know the joys and challenges of proclaiming the Word in any setting. This group includes priests who preside at Mass almost every day; pastors who preach regularly on the weekends; deacons who periodically preach at Mass and baptisms; theologians and religious educators who give witness talks at liturgies; and catechists who are designated to speak at children's liturgies. We hope that this material will be helpful also to seminary professors who teach homiletics and to their students, especially since it combines both theological perspectives and practical suggestions.

Kevin and I are both products of and active participants in the Catholic tradition. Our approach and language (for example, homily rather than sermon) reflect current developments within the Catholic community. Nevertheless, we believe this book can be of value to those who preach within other traditions: Orthodox, Anglican, mainstream Protestant, and evangelical. Our national survey was totally random, and our workshops have drawn Protestant participants from a wide variety of denominations.

Simply put, our purpose is to help preachers improve their critically important ministry of proclaiming the Word of God. This awesome task should move preachers to prayerful reflection and diligent preparation. There is a great fund of wisdom and practical knowledge residing in the heads and hearts of men and women who have the privilege of proclaiming the Word. Many do an outstanding job. None of us who preach, however, can rest satisfied with our current skills and level of performance. All of us can find ways to deepen our receptivity to God's Word and our ability to proclaim it. This ministry is too important to be stunted by complacency. Most weekends I wake up feeling vaguely anxious about the heavy responsibility of presiding at the liturgy and preaching the Word. Kevin tells me this anxiety can be transformed into a healthy catalyst for deeper prayer and better preparation—good advice for all who feel this burden.

The chapters in the book move from remote preparation for preaching to the actual delivery of homilies and evaluating them. The opening chapter explores the nature and importance of preaching, offering motivation for carrying out this ministry with enthusiasm and diligence. As disciples of Christ charged with the preaching ministry, we stand in a long line of men and women who have faithfully proclaimed the teaching of the Master in diverse historical and cultural settings. Chapter 2 invites a self-examination of what we can do to become better homilists. Preachers can benefit from a systematic plan for personal growth that looks for progress in the physical, emotional, imaginative, intellectual, moral, and religious dimensions of authentic human existence. It is also helpful to understand our own usual approach to preaching and the theology, perhaps implicit, that grounds it. Chapter 3 helps us develop a deeper understanding of the members of our congregations, who share a common human nature and are shaped by a variety of distinctive experiences: for example, living through the birth of the postmodern world; responding to cultural trends in the United States; and dealing with the threat of terrorism. We pay particular attention to the younger generations, who pose special challenges to preachers. Genuine service and careful listening provide the entree into the minds and hearts of the diverse individuals who make up our congregations.

Chapter 4 turns to the general task of engaging and interpreting the Scripture readings proclaimed at worship. We suggest a respectful and mutually critical conversation between the readings and the preacher who represents the congregation. Special attention is given to interpreting the gospel parables. The crucial fifth chapter, which draws on insights from the modern discipline of hermeneutics, offers a framework and many suggestions for determining the focus and function of the homily. Focus, as distinguished from theme, relates the message of the readings to the existential concerns of the congregation. It takes into account various contexts: the Bible as a whole, the particular book of the Bible, the whole liturgical year, the current liturgical cycle, and the worship celebration itself. Function has to do with the kind of transformation the homily is designed to accomplish: for example, a spiritual awakening or engagement in a social-justice activity. Chapter 6 offers practical suggestions for gathering material for the homily and organizing it into a coherent whole with a clear sequence of development. The proper use of stories is an important aspect of assembling material that gives witness and gains attention. Preaching at weddings and funerals presents special challenges, as does composing homilies on matters of justice and peace that can overcome congregational apathy and resistance. This final chapter also rehearses common suggestions for delivering better homilies and evaluating their effectiveness. The appendix contains a summary of the national survey we conducted as well as the results of our more recent local survey.

In writing these chapters I have drawn not only on my own experience as pastor and theologian but also on numerous books and articles explicitly dealing with preaching. Much of that material has melded together in my mind and is now not distinguishable from my own thought. Certain books stand out as helpful, however: *Preaching: The Art and the Craft* by Walter J. Burghardt (New York: Paulist, 1987); *Homiletic: Moves and Structures* by David Buttrick (Philadelphia: Fortress, 1987); *The Witness of Preaching* by Thomas G. Long (Louisville: Westminster John Knox, 1989); *Preaching* by Fred Craddock (Nashville: Abingdon, 1985); *Between Two Worlds* by John Scott (Grand Rapids: Eerdmans, 1982); *Interactive Preaching* by D. Stephenson Bond (St. Louis: CBP Press, 1981); *Naming Grace: Preaching and the Sacramental Imagination* by Mary Catherine Hilkert (New York: Continuum, 1997); and *Preaching Better: Practical Suggestions for Homilists* by Ken Untener (New York: Paulist, 1999).

We hope that the dialogue between pastor and psychologist that forms the core of this book will draw others into a fruitful conversation on ways to improve the preaching ministry in the early years of a new millennium.

KEVIN ANDERSON RESPONSE

Twenty years ago, after a period in the Jesuit novitiate, I had the good fortune of meeting James Bacik, who has been an important mentor and friend to me ever since. While doing a year of service at Jim's parish, I heard him preach often. I also had the remarkable opportunity to complete an individual guided study of the great books with Jim. Meeting weekly for an extended lunch, we discussed Plato, Aristotle, Augustine, Aquinas, Descartes, Kant, Kierkegaard, Nietzsche, Heidegger, Sartre, Barth, Tillich, Rahner, and others in a year-long feast of ideas. Spiritually and intellectually, Jim has been a light unto my path, and it has therefore been a privilege to collaborate with him on this project.

People in our community travel from far and wide to hear Jim shed light on the human condition and their personal spiritual paths. His knowledge of and ability to communicate engagingly about the deeply felt concerns that people carry in their hearts is what sets his approach to the preaching ministry apart. In our research studies on preaching, the results of which are described in detail in the appendix, Jim's listener-rated scores for preaching effectiveness were the highest of several dozen preachers studied in our community. This proclaimer of the Word is both a scholar who knows the theological dimension of the art and craft of preaching and an active pastor who practices what he preaches, both in life and in the pulpit.

Though I often do public speaking as a psychologist in workshops, my own experience of preaching is, to say the least, limited. While in the novitiate, I preached occasionally to the Jesuit community. In addition, I grew up participating in frequent home Masses with my uncle, the late Richard McCormick, SJ. Uncle Dick invariably used the dialogue homily format, so I grew up in a family community that valued reflecting on and applying the Word of God to life's joys and concerns.

Whereas Jim brings immense theological preparation and decades of dedication to the practice of preaching, I bring to this book three dimensions. First, I have been a keenly interested "consumer" of homilies for all of my adult life. I am always moved by a homily, but whether I am moved to spiritual insight, boredom, or even anger has much to do with the content and delivery of the homily. Just as Jim's approach to preaching is grounded in a deep appreciation for the human experience, his decision to include a listener as a coauthor of the book keeps this discussion of the preaching ministry grounded in its ultimate intent: impacting listeners. In responding to Jim's material in this book, I symbolize the spiritual hunger of all listeners to whom the preaching endeavor is directed.

Second, I bring an appreciation for the value of research and an understanding of the human mind and communication processes to the topic. To our knowledge, our research studies—

which included asking over two thousand listeners to rate approximately 150 preachers on thirty-six different variables—are unprecedented. Preaching is to the human soul what medicine is to the body or psychotherapy is to the psyche. Both medicine and psychotherapy are awash in thousands of research studies intended to guide practitioners in developing more effective approaches. The time has come for preaching to move beyond a narrow reliance on theory and idiosyncratic preaching styles. What works—that is, what connects with the listener's heart and moves him or her toward a fuller embrace of gospel values—can be studied rigorously and scientifically. The studies we conducted only hint at the wealth of knowledge that could be gained from a more scientific, systematic study of preaching. While our major objective is to provide input for practicing preachers, our first-of-a-kind research has broader implications for how knowledge of preaching can advance and how preachers are trained.

Third, the thousands of hours that I have spent listening to human concerns in the context of psychotherapy have made it clear to me that people in our consumer society are spiritually hungry. They have not managed to fill up their deepest longings with possessions, money, success, or other prizes held out by the culture as the motivating forces of life. People attend church hoping for their deep spiritual hunger to be nourished, and preaching is one of the primary ways in which this happens. Therefore, I have a deep respect for those who carry on the regular public reflection on spiritual matters that is preaching. An awareness of the crucial importance of preaching has motivated me to contribute whatever insights might help practitioners do it more effectively.

As we began the writing of this book, Jim encouraged me to use my "airtime" to respond to his writings in whatever way I felt appropriate. There was no attempt to ensure that our perspectives agreed at every turn. Just as the fields of medicine and psychotherapy never presume to declare that all is known or agreed upon, the discipline of preaching will be well served by the formulation and testing of various hypotheses about how preaching can be done most effectively. Fields advance by exploring often-competing ideas of how to proceed, and preaching is no exception.

For all those who participate in the ministry of shedding light on the path of the people in the pews week after week, I hope the theological, practical, and research-based material in this book will illuminate insights into how to preach effectively to human concerns.

It should be noted that throughout this book, I will make reference to "top ten" predictors of preaching effectiveness. These are the ten survey items that emerged from among thirty-six predictors as those most correlated with preacher ratings in our data. These top ten predictors from the three largest samples (which included nearly two thousand listener surveys) are the following:

1. This preacher's style of delivering the sermon helps keep my attention.
2. This preacher's sermons make me feel like he or she knows what is in my heart.
3. This preacher helps me get a new or deeper appreciation of the Scripture readings.
4. This preacher's sermons usually have a clear central message.
5. This preacher's sermons are relevant to my daily life.
6. This preacher makes creative use of stories and examples to enhance the sermon.
7. This preacher uses humor effectively in sermons.
8. This preacher usually presents ideas in the sermon very similar to my own.
9. This preacher is a very likable person.
10. This preacher knows the real struggles of life.

When a listener responded positively to the above items, it was likely that her or his evaluation of the preacher's effectiveness would also be positive. The higher an item's ranking on the above list, the more it correlated with preacher ratings (that is, the more knowledge of a listener's response to that item could help us predict his or her rating of the preacher's effectiveness). This top ten list should not be taken as the last word, but rather as the first word in a potentially long line of research. Our studies are only the proverbial tip of the iceberg of what can be learned about preaching using empirical methods. The appendix contains the details of our studies for interested readers.

JAMES BACIK RESPONSE

Kevin has a distinct perspective on preaching that will enrich the material in this book. He works well with symbols and imagery. He is the one who suggested the title *A Light Unto My Path* (Ps 119:115), and I expect that he will return to that image in his comments. I believe that his approach will make the main ideas in this book more concrete and accessible. We did study some of the great books together, and this gives us important shared reference points. Kevin also was a great help to me when I served as the writer for the committee of the Catholic bishops that produced the pastoral letter on campus ministry, *Empowered by the Spirit*. It was clear then that we were compatible theologically and could work together.

Kevin's positive comments about my own preaching are much appreciated and perhaps lend credibility to the approaches advocated. We can expect more criticisms and helpful additions in his responses to subsequent chapters. This format taps his excellent responsive skills, honed through his years as a therapist, and enables him to present his distinctive approaches and perspectives. I am counting on him to show how the statistical material generated by our national surveys can support and challenge the preaching ministry.

CHAPTER ONE

The Nature and Purpose of Preaching

"Father, I came here to Mass expecting to hear something in your sermon, and I listened carefully, but you never said anything." That comment, made to me early in my priesthood by a friendly and honest parishioner, Frank Newman, has remained in my mind for over forty years as an enduring reminder of the importance of the task of preaching. When tempted to neglect or delay my homily preparation, I hear Frank's voice reminding me that people gathering for liturgy expect and need to hear the Word of God proclaimed in an energizing and intelligible manner.

Challenge and Response

The contemporary world has generated new challenges to the traditional respect for preaching. A society that prizes individual freedom and open dialogue has problems with a form of communication that sounds preachy and one-sided. Deconstructionists, who espouse a total relativism, insist that sermons that propound a definite point of view are an unwarranted effort to exercise coercive power over a captive audience. The public scandals involving popular televangelists and priests guilty of sexual abuse have tinged preaching with a new suspicion of hypocrisy. Poor sermons help create a general sense that preaching is irrelevant. Critical parishioners commonly object that homilies are "up there," meaning that they are too abstract, theoretical, idealistic, complex, and out of touch with real life; or they are "back there," which suggests that they concentrate on the biblical world and historical events without showing what this means for life in the contemporary world. Many factors in today's world call into question the value and significance of the whole preaching ministry.

We need to respond to this by rooting the importance of preaching in the very nature of this specific ministry. Preaching is essentially the public proclamation of the Word of God in the community of faith. Homilists are called by God and the community to herald the good news of salvation, to announce the kingdom, to witness to the resurrection of Jesus, and to impart Christian wisdom. The purpose of preaching is to help hearers, as individuals and as a community, to appropriate the message of salvation and to live it out.

Theological Context

The nature and importance of the preaching ministry become clearer when placed in a larger theological context. The God of biblical faith is the sovereign Lord who speaks the Word that brings the whole of creation into existence and guides it to its fulfillment. God's Word is powerful and fruitful, like the rain that comes from the sky and fructifies the earth (Isa 55:7–11). The divine communication creates the material world as well as the finite spirits who can respond freely and intelligently. We human beings are essentially hearers of the Word. We have the root capacity to appropriate the divine message. Our hearts long for a Word from the Lord that can come to us only in our common history and in our individual experience. God's self-communication sustains and guides the whole universe. We live and move in a graced world. All things are potentially revelatory. Everything can mediate the divine Word to us.

The divine self-giving reached an unsurpassable high point in Jesus of Nazareth, the Word made flesh. He is the definitive prophet, who proclaims the presence and the ultimate completion of the reign of God. In word and deed he announced the good news of salvation. He was at the same time the great hearer of the Word, the exemplar of full humanity as well as the parable of the Father, the Word of God personally present for us.

Jesus gathered a group of disciples and gave them the task of preaching the good news. The risen Christ commissioned individuals like Mary of Magdala, Peter, and Paul of Tarsus to give witness to the saving power of his new glorified life. The task of the whole church is to keep the memory of Jesus alive, to announce the good news, to proclaim the Word of God. In fidelity to this task, the community of faith officially calls and prepares individuals to preach the Word and to encourage all the baptized to give witness to their faith. This is indeed a high calling, a noble task, a challenging responsibility. The preaching ministry has an intrinsic importance and an essential value that runs deeper than criticisms, scandals, and poor homilies.

We who preach today stand in a long line of those who accepted the call to speak about the things of God. We are disciples of Jesus, who showed us the way by going about preaching the gospel of the kingdom (Matt 9:35). Faithful to the call of their Master, the apostles gave a high priority to preaching, devoting themselves "to prayer and to serving the word" (Acts 6:4). Guided by his experience of the risen Lord, Paul refused to claim his preaching ministry as a reason for boasting; rather, he understood it as a divinely imposed obligation that he willingly accepted (1 Cor 9:16–17). He carried on his task in fear and much trembling, but with great confidence, not in the persuasive power of his own arguments but in the power of God revealed in Jesus Christ crucified (1 Cor. 2:1–5). Most of us can identify with Paul's fear and trembling before the awesome task of preaching regularly. Our challenge is to follow his example of complete reliance on the power of God and the wisdom of the gospel.

Great Preachers

Throughout Christian history, men and women have carried on the preaching ministry with great dedication, skill, and courage. John Chrysostom (347–407), a bishop and doctor of the church, is recognized as the patron saint of preachers because of his elegant and courageous preaching. He wrote commentaries on Paul as well as the Gospels of Matthew and John, stressing their literal meaning and practical applications. As Patriarch of Constantinople, he lived a simple lifestyle while denouncing from the pulpit the luxurious lives of the royal court and the upper class. For this courageous witness to the gospel he was exiled from his see and died as a result of subsequent hardships. He became known as a "martyr of the pulpit" and remains for us a challenging reminder of our call to preach the gospel with courage despite opposition.

Hildegard of Bingen (1098–1179) was a Benedictine sister who served as superior of a small community. At the age of forty-two she had a profound religious experience that unleashed a remarkable surge of creative energy. She saw a brilliant, heavenly vision and heard the voice of the "Living Light" instructing her to "speak those things which you see and hear." As a result, she wrote nine books and composed a whole cycle of original chants and songs for the liturgical year. In 1158 the emperor Frederic Barbarossa invited her to undertake a public preaching tour on behalf of church reform. For the next twelve years, she traveled all over Europe preaching to the clergy as well as the laity in great cathedrals and numerous monasteries. Hildegard reminds us today of the important contributions made to the preaching ministry by women as well as the common call to draw on our own experience of the things of God we have seen and heard.

Closer to our own time, we find inspiration in Oscar Romero, archbishop of San Salvador (1912–1980), another martyr of the pulpit, who courageously proclaimed a prophetic word against the injustices suffered by his people and was assassinated as he presided at the Eucharist on March 24, 1980. The courageous preachers throughout history remind us of the remarkable power of the Word of God to challenge the entrenched and to liberate the captives.

Both theology and historical practice illumine the true nature of preaching. A homily is a proclamation of the Word of God, not an academic lecture. It is a witness to gospel truth, not a psychological analysis. Preaching takes place within a community of faith and is not a private activity. It draws on the Christian tradition and is not an expression of personal opinion. A sermon makes the Word present for current reflection and is not a nostalgic trip into the past. It judges the current situation in the light of the Christian tradition and does not simply baptize the current culture. Liturgical homilies are organically connected with the Eucharist; they are not separate events. Authentic preaching is always the proclamation of the Word of God within the community of faith for the purpose of personal and community transformation. As such it possesses an intrinsic worth and enduring importance.

The Protestant traditions have performed a valuable service by putting such great emphasis on the sermon in the public worship of the church. For Catholics, the Second Vatican Council brought to focus a renewed appreciation of the nature and significance of preaching. Just as Christ was sent by the Father, so he sent the apostles, filled with the Holy Spirit, to preach the gospel to every creature and to proclaim liberty from the power of evil through his resurrection (*Sacrosanctum concilium* 6). All the preaching of the church should be rooted and nourished by sacred Scripture, a living and active Word that builds up the community of faith (*Dei verbum* 21). By proclaiming the gospel, the church incorporates the hearers into Christ so they can grow to full maturity (*Lumen gentium* 17). The primary duty of ordained priests, as coworkers of the bishops, is to preach the gospel and to proclaim the mysteries of Christ. To accomplish this often-difficult task, preachers must expound the Word of God not in an abstract and general way but by applying the truth of the gospel to the current circumstances of life. The homily finds its fullest expression as an organic part of the eucharistic celebration, where Christians find their nourishment and guidance (*Presbyterorum ordinis* 4). This brief survey of conciliar teaching makes it clear that preaching is not a peripheral activity but a primary responsibility of the ordained clergy.

Numerous images and metaphors illumine the nature of preaching. Within the New Testament, preaching is seen primarily as handing on the Word of God. The Second Letter to Timothy presents Paul as one appointed to be a herald of the gospel, much as a servant would make a public announcement on behalf of his king (1:11). Paul sees himself as an ambassador for Christ, as if God were appealing through him (2 Cor 5:20). As heralds or ambassadors, we preach not our own message but the

Word of God that has been entrusted to us. Reflecting on the parable of the sower and the seed, we can see ourselves as ones chosen by God to disseminate his Word as widely as possible, realizing that we do not have control of how the message is received (Luke 8:4–15). Applying a striking image in Matthew's Gospel, we are charged by Christ to shout boldly and enthusiastically from the housetop what we have heard whispered in our prayerful encounters with him (10:27).

Some images of preaching highlight the importance of proclaiming the Word to the congregation in their specific situation. The craft of preaching demands bridge building, constructing smooth and helpful connections between the gospel and the people who thirst for the Word. Preachers are wounded healers who can empathize with the painful struggles of their people and who know personally the healing power of the Word. Effective preachers are good storytellers who know how to relate the normative story of Jesus to the stories lived out by the hearers of the Word. Homilists are witnesses to the power of the gospel, making available to the congregation what they know from experience to be true. They are exegetes or interpreters who can discern the deeper meanings of biblical texts and explain them to people today.

Some metaphors for preaching emphasize the task of recognizing and illuminating the graced condition of hearers of the Word. Preachers are midwives who help bring forth the divine life already present in the community of faith and its individual members. Homilists are like poets who can express in colorful language and lively metaphors the way the congregation participates in the death and rising of Christ. We are mystagogues who help people get in touch with the mystery dimension of human existence, and who show how the Christian message illumines all aspects of our experience.

The great diversity of these images reminds us that proclaiming the Word immerses us in the ultimately mysterious relationship between God and the human family—a relationship that can be viewed from multiple perspectives and is not exhausted by a simple definition. Taken together, these images point to the tremendous importance of preaching, an activity that makes

God's saving Word available and responds to such vital human needs.

Standing in the line of great preachers such as Origen, Augustine, Aquinas, and Luther, the neo-orthodox theologian Karl Barth (1886–1968) gave eloquent expression to the importance of preaching when he claimed "that there is nothing more important, urgent, helpful, redemptive, salutary and relevant than speaking and hearing the word of God." We probably all know days when this lofty praise of preaching sounds intimidating. At those times, it is crucial to remember that we are servants of the Word of God, who chooses to work with weak and limited instruments. It is also helpful to recall the Frank Newmans in our congregation, those who come to worship needing and expecting to hear something from the pulpit—real persons with distinctive faces who are looking for a word of encouragement, guidance, inspiration, motivation, challenge, and hope. They deserve our best efforts to make available the Word of God with its remarkable power to heal, transform, and liberate.

KEVIN ANDERSON RESPONSE

I remember a homily I heard at a wedding over twenty years ago. The priest had one simple message: *Make new mistakes.* "Your marriage," he said, "will include some mistakes—just don't make the same old mistakes that your parents or their parents made." This one line, which he repeated over and over throughout the homily with much enthusiasm—comes back to me frequently and I have shared it with many clients. I suspect that this is what most preachers hope for: to make a useful and memorable impact on those who hear them speak. Preaching is not only a regular dose of spiritual input or training. When done well, it can change the course and quality of people's lives and awaken them to a more active engagement with their own spiritual development.

In highlighting the unique importance of preaching and by providing metaphors for the role of the preacher (wounded healer, storyteller, midwife, poet, mystagogue), Jim spurred a number of reactions in me. I have grouped these under five headings: *wisdom, witness, grace, creativity,* and *centrality.*

Wisdom

Jim writes that the function of the preacher is to impart Christian wisdom. Though we often think of wisdom in a cumulative sense—what a person gathers throughout a lifetime—the first definition of the word is "knowledge and experience needed to make sensible decisions and judgments." This is what those who listen to preaching long for—ideas, insights, stories, humor, anything that will help them better understand the joyful and difficult aspects of their lives and continue to take steps toward spiritual growth. When we say that preaching is fundamentally about imparting wisdom, this implies that it is not mainly about giving a history lesson, teaching catechism, or delivering a theological lecture. In stating that many homilies are too "up there" or "back there," Jim has neatly summarized what I and many listeners feel all too often. When churchgoers talk about preachers, one of the first words to come up is *relevance*. What we want is wisdom—a light to help us find God in whatever joyful or challenging experiences are occurring in our lives. We tune out very quickly if we sense we're not going to hear anything with meaningful implications for our daily lives. This is backed up by our research, which found that about half of the variability in how listeners rate preachers can be predicted by whether the listener finds the homily relevant to daily life (see data on survey item "This preacher's sermons are relevant to my daily life" in the appendix).

In reflecting on the task of imparting wisdom, one of the first realizations is that sharing wisdom requires a preacher to be a person in an active and lifelong process of scouring for insight wherever he or she can find it. Just as a writer can know the rules of grammar but only makes a mark on the world of literature if she or he has something worthwhile to write about, learning the mechanics of delivering a good homily is a necessary but insufficient condition for effective preaching. In collaboration with a friend, I once created a cartoon in which a frog was sitting in a therapist's office saying, "No offense, Dr. Tad Pole, but I was thinking of working with someone a little bit ahead of me on the journey." Listeners feel the same way about preachers. Personal development is crucial to a preacher's honing his or her whole mind and spirit for the task of imparting spiritual wisdom to the congregation. We will have more to say on the importance of personal development in chapter 2.

Witness

In referring to preaching as a "witness," Jim led me to think of the witness talks that laypeople give at Marriage Encounters, retreats, or parish missions. A "witness talk" involves some personal sharing of one's experience of life and what has been learned from it. I think Jim and I differ on this point, but I feel that too few preachers reveal anything meaningful about their own spiritual journeys to listeners. Our data indicate that judicious use of personal information can enhance preaching effectiveness. About 25 percent of variability in listeners' ratings of preachers can be accounted for by their response to the item, "This preacher shares significant personal experiences in sermons." On average, the stronger the positive response to this question, the stronger the rating of the preacher's effectiveness. This does not mean that personal disclosure by the preacher *causes* people to experience homilies as effective. It only tells us that there is some association between personal sharing and positive ratings of preaching. (All of the data in our studies is correlational; that is, it demonstrates associations between variables but does not indicate that one variable causes another.)

It is safer to talk about the spiritual life in general than actually to witness to it in a personal way. There is a fine line here, because a homily is not intended as a place for a preacher to place undue emphasis on his or her own life or share inappropriate details. But listeners want to *know that you know* about real life. What psychologists call "universality" is the awakening that comes with realizing, "I thought I was alone in that particular difficulty, but I'm not." This can be accomplished to some degree by talking about what you've learned by serving people as a minister, but I believe that tactful personal self-disclosure also can be engaging and make homilies more memorable. Listeners won't experience a preacher as a wounded healer unless the preacher has

the courage to share some of the difficulties she or he has encountered on the spiritual path. Of all the homilies I have heard Jim
preach, the one that affected me most profoundly was his personal
sharing, at his mother's funeral, of her practice of the virtue of
acceptance of hardship in their family experience. His personal
witness impacted me deeply in a way that a safer or less heartfelt
treatment of the topic would not have.

Grace

How good it was to read in Jim's comments that "we live and
move in a graced world. All things are potentially revelatory."
This idea has been at the core of my spirituality for years, yet I
rarely hear it expressed in homilies. I believe this concept is
important because most of those who attend religious services in
our culture have developed a disintegrated spirituality. By this I
mean that we are prone to think of spirituality as what happens in
church or in formal religious activities. Many people go to church
to be filled up with an experience of God, rather than to celebrate
or reflect on an experience of God that is an integral part of their
daily lives. One critical role of the preacher is to help people
become spiritually integrated again—to assist listeners in expand-
ing their ideas about where and how God can be experienced.
When we rehearse over and over only familiar doctrines or ideas
about God, spiritual growth stagnates. The terms *midwife* and
mystagogue intrigued me as challenging metaphors for the
preacher's task of helping listeners develop an authentic and integrated spirituality.

Creativity

In order to help listeners integrate God-awareness into daily
life, preachers need to approach their task creatively. The human
brain responds to new ideas with far greater interest than to old
ones. This is an innate human tendency that is evident shortly
after birth. Newborns, for instance, look at new stimuli much

longer than at things with which they are already familiar. No matter how good it is, I rarely want to see a movie repeatedly, because my brain would always rather discover a new story than review an old one. Thus, Jim's emphasis on storytelling is right on target. Storytelling engages the mind and presents material in ways than can create new connections in the brain of the listener.

Our data support the importance of creativity in preaching. About half of the variability in listeners' ratings of preachers can be predicted by their response to the item "This preacher makes creative use of stories and examples to enhance the sermon." The item "This preacher makes use of valuable insights from other sources such as poetry, literature, psychology, or philosophy" is also positively correlated with ratings of preacher effectiveness.

I think one aspect of creative preaching that is too often overlooked is the importance of striving for a poetic touch in one's speaking. If the homilist who said "Make new mistakes" had said something like, "Try to be aware of doing things a bit differently from the people you lived with growing up," it would not have lodged in my brain the way the briefer and more poetic phrase did. If Franklin Roosevelt had said, "We don't have anything to be concerned about except the actual experience of being afraid," it would not be so well remembered as his famous "We have nothing to fear but fear itself." It's not realistic to expect all preachers to become great poets or readers of literature, but preachers are engaged in a task similar to the writer's: communicating so as to move the listener or reader. Just as it is a bit too convenient in the spiritual life to claim that ordinary people can't strive for the holiness of the saints, it is too easy for preachers to deny their call to speak to spiritual needs with the eloquence of poets. An appreciation of the power of language is essential in delivering a message that will have the desired impact and be memorable.

Centrality

I agree completely with Jim that preaching is central, not peripheral, to a minister's role in society. When Catholic parishioners talk about where they attend services, the quality of the preaching is usually the first item discussed. Because the rest of the liturgy is quite familiar, the homily stands out as the one element of the communal worship that provides an opportunity for creative imparting of spiritual wisdom.

Preaching is the primary ongoing public forum in which spiritual matters are addressed in our culture. Just as physicians and psychologists are required to take continuing education courses to remain current in their fields, it is vital that preachers make every effort to improve their abilities. Beyond individual preachers continuing to develop their skills, the field of preaching needs an influx of evidence-based research that can provide clearer guidance on what does and does not connect with the human spirit in the preaching encounter. Of the thirty-six variables that we studied in over two thousand surveys of listeners, two rose to the top as most important: *the ability to keep the listener's attention* and *the ability to make listeners feel that the speaker "knows what is in my heart"* (see appendix). These two variables taken together were able to account for approximately 70 to 85 percent of the variability in preacher effectiveness scores across the various listener samples. This means that if one wants to know how a preacher will be rated (effective or ineffective), we can predict with 70- to 85-percent accuracy based on "keeping attention" and "knows what is in my heart." This research is only a beginning—many more studies like this need to be funded and their results translated into more effective training of preachers. The role of preaching is too important to continue to allow it to proceed uninformed by high-quality studies of what works and what does not.

JAMES BACIK RESPONSE

I am not yet sure whether Kevin and I really disagree on the use of personal stories in homilies—I prefer to address the question more comprehensively in chapter 6, on composing the homily. I do know that personal stories can end up putting undue emphasis on the preacher. In a homily stressing practical charity, I tried to highlight the kindness of a good Samaritan who gave me a ride to an airport. The story context went like this. I was driving from Toledo to the Detroit airport when a couple of miles from the airport my car broke down. I was already pressed for time to catch the only possible flight to Los Angeles, where I was scheduled to give a talk to a large number of priests. So I left the car on the side of the road and began hitchhiking. A kind gentleman picked me up almost immediately, drove out of his way to get me to the airport, and declined any money to pay for his efforts—a real good example of the kind of concrete charity taught by Jesus. The reaction from many people to the story, however, focused on me. What happened to your car? Weren't you afraid to hitchhike? You certainly get to travel a lot. No one commented on the good deed or connected the story with the purpose of the homily.

In the homily at my mother's funeral I did include personal references that stressed acceptance as a key to an authentic Christian life. When my mother was in the dying process, I tried to commiserate with her: "Mom you don't have much control over things in your life anymore." Weakened physically yet still mentally alert, she responded pointedly: "That's right, I don't have control over anything, and, James, neither do you." Judging by Kevin's response to the homily, you could conclude that this personal story helped further the purpose of the homily. We will return to this question in chapter 6.

CHAPTER TWO

Preaching and Personal Development

Preachers who appreciate the fundamental importance of pro-claiming the Word recognize a corresponding call to personal growth and professional development. By its very nature, preach-ing is personally involving. It is a ministry that calls for commit-ment, not a job that can be done dispassionately. The character of the preacher has an influence on the effectiveness of the homily. Congregations are turned off by repeated patterns of glib talk, inauthentic speech, and poor preparation. They find enlighten-ment and encouragement from preachers who wrestle with the great questions and are serious about their spiritual growth. Preaching is most effective when it flows from a self-sacrificing life of service to the community. In short, remote preparation for preaching demands attention to personal development.

Systematic Personal Development

All personal growth is a gift from God. Sometimes we make progress beyond expectation and without apparent effort. At other times, growth occurs as a graced result of a specific strategy and systematic effort. One strategy is to develop the virtues and personal characteristics commonly recognized as important for effective proclamation: faith that involves a personal commitment to Christ and regular immersion in Scripture and prayer; compas-sion that moves us to suffer with people who are hurting; personal integrity that is honest, authentic, natural, and humane; selfless love that cares for others and rises above egotism; and a sense of humor that reveals a light touch and a healthy perspective on the limitations of life.

A preacher can also use the liturgical year as a catalyst for a structured approach to spiritual growth: for example, Advent invites growth in the virtue of hope; the Christmas season is a time to sharpen our awareness of the presence of Christ in the world; Lent demands an intelligently chosen penance; the Easter season offers opportunities to deepen our relationship with the risen Christ. This strategy has the advantage of providing an experiential basis for preaching during these seasons.

Borrowing a framework from the Catholic theologian Bernard Lonergan, we can work at personal development in the various dimensions of our lives: physical, emotional, imaginative, intellectual, moral, and religious. Preaching requires energy in preparation and delivery, and so remote preparation demands attention to proper eating patterns, adequate sleep, and regular exercise. Sleep-deprived pastors find it harder to prepare, and out-of-shape preachers may feel lethargic. Modern medicine confirms the traditional wisdom that there is an essential connection between the health of the body and the health of the mind. Spirituality is rooted in bodiliness. Getting ourselves in better physical shape can improve our self-esteem and our performance in the pulpit.

Emotional Growth

A preacher who is emotionally balanced and integrated is less likely to impede the intrinsic power of the Word of God. Unexamined feelings, such as repressed anger, hidden envy, and internal prejudices, can easily surface in the preparation and delivery of a homily. If we misread the real sources of our own joys and satisfactions, our preaching is less likely to sound authentic. Guilt feelings can keep preachers from addressing important, sensitive issues. Emotional growth requires being in touch with feelings, naming them accurately and mobilizing them for constructive action. As preachers we can make progress by paying attention to our emotional responses to the people we serve and to the Scripture texts proclaimed in worship.

For example, a homilist finds that he is unusually agitated as he prepares a homily on the parable of workers who were paid the same wage for one hour of labor as those who bore the heat of a long day. Taking time for prayerful reflection on his strong emotional reaction, he gradually comes to see that the root of his agitation is envy. He is upset because some of his parishioners enjoy a luxurious lifestyle, although they do not work nearly as hard as he does. This helpful, if embarrassing, insight leads him to a long and disciplined effort to accept graciously the realities of his ministerial vocation, which has its own emotional and spiritual satisfactions. Preachers who have struggled to achieve a reflective and integrated affective life are better prepared to deliver homilies that resonate in the hearts of the congregation.

Imaginative Growth

A fertile imagination is a great resource for proclaiming a gripping and compelling message. Imagination enables us to make linkages across time by bringing past events into the present and by envisioning a future different from the present. We can reminisce and we can dream. As imaginative beings, we can appreciate the power of symbol, myth, and ritual to illumine the deeper dimensions of life. Imagination allows us to detect the clues to the divine presence in our daily lives. It gives us an intuitive feel for the signals of light and hope in the midst of the darkness that threatens us. Our imaginations are like a radar screen that scans our common history and our personal experience for significant images and preserves them as repositories of meaning. Human beings have the creative capacity to combine these images into new patterns, to develop metaphors and analogies, to compose poems, to tell stories, and to create rituals. As the philosopher Paul Ricoeur says, the symbol gives birth to thought. Imagination grounds the work of intellect.

Preaching that lacks imagination strikes congregations as dull, lifeless, and boring. It tends to be either overly cerebral or merely emotional, too rationalistic or too sentimental. As homilists, we have the task of relating the stories of grace drawn from contemporary experience to the stories of grace found in the Bible and the Christian tradition. This demands attention to the symbols, images, and metaphors that point to the mystery dimension of ordinary life. It includes the ability to discern common characteristics in human experience and to describe them accurately and vividly. The art of preaching is to discern those parts of the great Christian symbol system that best illumine and judge specific aspects of contemporary experience. Effective preachers find creative ways to tell the story of Jesus so that it reveals grace at work in the world today and unmasks the demonic powers that threaten us.

Some preachers are born poets or storytellers who can simply draw on their God-given talents to deliver homilies that stir the imagination. The rest of us need to work at developing our more limited skills. A good starting point is to listen more carefully to how our people describe their own experience, especially attentive to striking images and symbols. We also need to be more alert to the symbolic material in our own experience. Our daydreams, which are more accessible than night dreams, sometimes suggest vivid ways of describing the deepest longings of the human heart. The Scripture readings for a given occasion often contain powerful images, apt metaphors, and memorable phrases that can be used in the homily. Reading good poetry and fiction nourishes the imagination, as does immersion in the world of art, music, and the theater. Preachers who take the time to develop their imaginations find that it pays off in more effective homilies.

Intellectual Growth

A preacher who is growing intellectually through the study of Scripture, theology, and related disciplines is better prepared to proclaim a fresh and challenging Word. Our homilies must appeal to intellect as well as to emotion and imagination—we need to have something to say. I recall a priest saying that his homilies had become boring to himself. He had no new ideas, no fresh perspectives to excite himself or the congregation. At the beginning of the twenty-first century, we are blessed with the remarkable advances made in Scripture studies and theology during the past century. Scripture scholars such as Reginald Fuller and Raymond Brown made results of modern critical studies widely available to preachers. The great Protestant theologians Karl Barth and Paul

Tillich, along with the Catholic giants Karl Rahner, Bernard Lonergan, and Hans Urs von Balthasar, refocused and reinterpreted the rich Christian heritage, providing marvelous resources for personal growth and effective preaching. Many other theologians have taken the seminal insights of these great thinkers and put them in a more popular form. Despite the ready availability of these materials, many preachers do not make use of them. Some think they are too busy to sort through this mass of material, not even knowing where to start. Others ignore these resources on the mistaken belief that they are irrelevant.

Karl Rahner insists that the more scientific theology is, the more pastorally relevant it is. Good solid theology, rooted in the rich Christian tradition and in touch with the questions of the age, offers a resource for preachers too valuable to be dismissed or neglected. Busy preachers should make intellectual growth a high priority and schedule around it.

Most of us cannot wade through the massive volumes produced by the giants. Some of their most valuable insights, however, are available also in their shorter and more popular works. Collections of homilies can be helpful: for example, *The New Being* by Paul Tillich (New York: Scribner, 1955); *The Great Church Year* by Karl Rahner (New York: Crossroad, 1993); *Light of the Word* by Hans Urs von Balthasar (San Francisco: Ignatius Press, 1993). General surveys of Scripture, such as Raymond Brown's *Introduction to the New Testament* (New York: Doubleday, 1997), are useful. At some point in our theological growth, we need a comprehensive view of the faith, an overview that allows us to see how the various points fit into our organic whole. The *Summa* of Thomas Aquinas did that for the medieval world, as did the *Institutes* of John Calvin for the Reformation period. The manageable contemporary summaries include *Systematic Theology* by Paul Tillich (Chicago: University of Chicago Press, 1951–63); *The Foundations of Christian Faith* by Karl Rahner (New York: Crossroad, 1982); *Principles of Christian Theology* by John Macquarrie (London: SCM Press, 1966); *On Being a Christian* by Hans Küng (Garden City, NY: Image Books, 1984); and *Dogmatics in Outline* by Karl Barth (New York: Philosophical Library, 1949). It is difficult to preach effectively on particular aspects of the

Christian message without having a sense of how they fit into the tradition as a whole.

Reading journals regularly is one way of staying current and coming up with new ideas. The *New Theology Review* connected with Catholic Theological Union of Chicago and Washington is written especially for pastors and has a regular feature on preaching. *Interpretation*, a quarterly published by Union Theological Seminary in Richmond, Virginia, provides a similar service. Many preachers keep up-to-date by reading periodicals such as *Christianity Today*, *America*, *Christian Century*, and *Commonweal*. Preachers will also benefit from composing short creeds for themselves and their congregations that express the essence of the Christian message in contemporary language. This exercise prompts deeper reflection on the core truths of the faith and how they relate to life today. Without some systematic effort at intellectual growth, we are in danger of preaching homilies that are boring to others and perhaps even to ourselves.

Moral Growth

By its very nature, preaching calls homilists to moral conversion, to pursue goodness and virtue rather than expediency and selfishness. The gospel we announce invites all believers to give generously of themselves out of a spirit of love, rather than merely observing the law out of fear. The Christian message demands that we reject the ethical relativism rampant in our culture in favor of a life of responsible freedom, which takes into account traditional wisdom as well as the divine summons to follow our conscience. Today we are more aware of the scriptural mandate to work for justice and peace in a world constricted by social sin and the oppressive power of unjust institutions.

Many preachers are painfully aware of the glaring gap between the high ideals we proclaim and our actual performance. None of us can claim perfection as a witness to Christ. We need a way to come to terms with our limitations and sins so that we can still preach with integrity and without paralyzing guilt. For our own peace of mind, it is important that we continue to strive for moral growth. Our conscience rests easier when we are making specific efforts to narrow the gap between gospel ideals and our actual behavior, conscious of both our total dependence on God's mercy and our own unavoidable limitations. Moral growth requires the cultivation of virtues that are like a second nature—virtues that enable us to respond fittingly in changing circumstances. Through well-chosen disciplines and the repetition of fitting behavior, we can gradually replace vices with virtues that enable us to choose the good with delight and relative ease.

The recovery of a virtue-centered approach to morality has been a healthy development in contemporary theology. Virtue stands in the middle between destructive extremes. Traditionally, the cardinal virtues of prudence, justice, temperance, and fortitude have provided a path to moral growth. Prudence is a practical moral wisdom that enables us to discern in specific situations the most fitting means to move closer to God, the goal of our journey. Today we are more aware that justice, which inclines us to give everyone their due, must include special care for those most in need and collaborative efforts to transform unjust systems and institutions. Fortitude or courage moves us to endure physical and emotional hardships and to overcome fears in living out the Christian life. Temperance, developed through discipline, inclines us to enjoy the pleasures of life in a reasonable way so that they bring us closer to God.

As Aquinas demonstrated in his *Summa*, the whole project of moral growth can be guided by the development of these cardinal virtues, especially when they are informed and guided by a charity that directs us to wholehearted love of God and love of neighbor as ourselves. Growth in any of these virtues moves us toward the kind of integrity that enriches our preaching. Virtues are developed through practice and disciplined effort. Even tiny steps toward becoming a more prudent, just, courageous, temperate, and loving person can give us confidence that we are moving in the right direction and can proclaim the Word with a measure of authenticity.

Religious Growth for Christians

Finally, preachers grow religiously by developing a deeper relationship with the great God. Religious development takes us from a false sense of self-sufficiency to a greater dependence on

God. We put aside selfish interests and make God our ultimate concern. We surrender ourselves to the Mystery who alone can satisfy the longings of our hearts. Our center of gravity shifts from ourselves to the God who, paradoxically, inhabits the very center of our being.

To grow religiously is to fall more deeply in love with our heavenly Father. For us Christians, the process of religious conversion is focused and mediated by Jesus Christ. Commitment to Christ means that we accept him as the final prophet and dedicate ourselves to following his example and teaching in our daily lives. As the living parable of divine love, Jesus reminds us that self-surrender places us in the arms of the God who is totally trustworthy. As the exemplar of fulfilled humanity, he demonstrates that complete dependence on God leads to greater freedom and growth. The risen Christ sends the Paraclete to illumine our journey and guide our ministry of the Word.

A Christ-centered spirituality has a trinitarian character that affects all the dimensions of our lives. When we think of our bodies as temples of the Holy Spirit, we are more inclined to take proper care of them. Mobilizing our emotions for constructive action is easier when we reflect on the affective life of Jesus, who knew compassion, sadness, and anger. A positive image of God as loving and compassionate prompts a healthy self-image and liberates our creative powers. The Spirit guides our intellectual development as we reflect on Christ as the wisdom of the Father. For us, moral growth is focused on love of God and neighbor, prompted by the Spirit and guided by the example of Jesus. Deepening our relationship to Christ opens our hearts to the call of the Father and the promptings of the Spirit. Growth in any of these dimensions will have a positive effect, directly or indirectly, on our preaching.

Professional Development

Our remote preparation for preaching includes not only personal growth but also professional development of our homiletic skills. Those of us who preach regularly have developed our own characteristic approaches: drawing on particular authors, stressing favorite biblical teachings, developing certain themes, employing a dominant methodology, and presenting particular perspectives. Our preaching reflects our theology, whether developed or unformed. We have our own ways of thinking about human nature, God, grace, revelation, salvation, Jesus Christ, the church, sacraments, the moral life, and the afterlife. Becoming more aware of the contours of our theology is an important step in preparing ourselves for more effective preaching. Unreflected preaching practice is in danger of falling into predictable patterns and narrow approaches that constrict the inherent power of the Word. A deeper understanding of the strengths and limitations of our own theology opens the way to homilies that better manifest the richness of the tradition and meet the needs of the congregation.

Classical and Contemporary Theology

Using a distinction developed by Bernard Lonergan, we can ask ourselves if our theology tends to be more classical or contemporary. Classical theology adopts a fixed or static perspective that emphasizes the timeless character of religious truth. Typically, it works from the top down, beginning with the scriptures or the Christian tradition and applying them to the human situation, and it emphasizes the transcendence of God, the divinity of Jesus, the gratuity of grace, the unique character of revelation, and the authority of the church.

Contemporary theology, in contrast, makes use of a dynamic standpoint and recognizes multiple perspectives that reveal various aspects of God's infinite truth. This theology is open to working from the bottom up, by taking human experience seriously as a starting point for reflection and a source of revelatory truth. Theologians with a contemporary mind-set tend to stress the immanence of God, the humanity of Jesus, the universality of grace, the variety of revelatory experiences, and the pluralism of views within the church. Contemporary theology is pluralistic, encompassing process theologians, transcendental Thomists, and a great variety of liberation thinkers.

In our workshops on preaching, some homilists clearly identify themselves as operating out of either a classical or a contemporary theology, but others see themselves moving from one approach to the other, depending on circumstances. Each approach has strengths and weaknesses. Classical preaching delivers a clear and definite message, but one must work hard to make sure the message connects with the experience of the congregation. Good contemporary preaching usually resonates with the hearers, but one must remember that the gospel stands in judgment on contemporary culture and current human experience.

Karl Barth and Dialectical Preaching

We can gain a more precise understanding of our implicit theology by examining the approach of seminal thinkers who remain influential today. Karl Barth, clearly a giant of twentieth-century theology, served as a pastor in the Swiss Reformed Church. He was passionate about the preaching ministry but became very dissatisfied with the approach advocated by the liberal Protestant professors who taught him theology. Barth's desire to become a more faithful preacher led him to an intense study of Paul's Letter to the Romans and the publication of his famous work *The Epistle to the Romans* (1918), which, in the words of Karl Adam, "fell like a bomb on the playground of the theologians." This book, which remains a classic expression of his early thought, is a powerful critique of any liberal tendency to reduce God to human proportions. For the early Barth, God is the "Wholly Other," the transcendent One who stands in strict judgment on the guilt of this world. The true God is "distinguished qualitatively from men and from everything human, and must never be identified with anything we name or experience, or conceive, or worship as God." It is only through Jesus Christ that we have access to God. Jesus is the prophet who sets before us "the complete strangeness of the Wholly Other" and exposes "the gulf which separates God and man." We cannot reach God by any human means: not through reason, with its philosophical arguments; not through feelings or religious sentiments; not through experience of nature or other persons. Our hope for revelation is founded entirely on the atoning death and resurrection of Jesus Christ, who alone bridges the gap between God and us. The historical Jesus refused to identify himself with any particular group or program. Standing in sovereign freedom against all the demonic forces and all the ideals erected by human pride, Jesus Christ and no other is our victorious leader.

Guided by this understanding of Jesus, Barth mounted a vigorous attack on Adolf Hitler soon after his inauguration as chancellor of Germany. He castigated church ministers who accepted an easy alliance between the gospel and the National Socialism espoused by Hitler. For refusing allegiance to Hitler, Barth was expelled from Germany and took a teaching post at the University of Basel, where he continued to attack Nazi ideology and to write his multivolume work *Church Dogmatics*. Although Barth later modified some of his views, it is the early Barth who best exemplifies what is commonly called a dialectical style of preaching. In the Catholic community this general approach is represented by Hans Urs von Balthasar (1905–1988), who wrote an important commentary on Barth and emphasized the splendor and beauty of God's revelation uniquely manifested in the supreme icon, Jesus Christ.

Dialectical preaching emphasizes the transcendence of God, who is Lord of creation and Judge of the world. It regards the revelation of God in Jesus Christ as surprising and unexpected and maintains that we are called to accept the unique truth of Christ not because it makes sense or accords with human nature; indeed, we believe in this truth in spite of its strange and paradoxical character. This style of preaching invites us to enter the world of the Bible, which is the normative witness to Jesus the Son of God. The New Testament presents a way of living that challenges accepted social standards and cultural norms. Dialectical preaching stresses judgment upon the world and salvation through Christ. It does not include much material from disciplines such as philosophy, psychology, economics, and sociology, nor does it borrow insights from other religious traditions. Rather, it tries to draw the hearer into the biblical world by focusing attention on the essential, unambiguous message of Christ.

Dialectical preaching is not easily seduced by the latest fads, current cultural trends, accepted social norms, or nationalistic arrogance. It presents the gospel of Christ as clear judgment on all contemporary idol making. On the other hand, it must deal with the danger of sounding irrelevant, confined to the ancient world without clear reference to current concerns. Rudolf Bultmann (1884–1976) recognized this problem and used the categories and language of existential philosophy, especially from Martin Heidegger, to make dialectical preaching more relevant to modern people who find the biblical world foreign to their experience.

Karl Rahner and Sacramental Preaching

Karl Rahner (1904–1984), the influential German Jesuit theologian, represents a very different style of preaching, one that can be described as correlational and sacramental. This approach is somewhat familiar to those in the Protestant world through the great Lutheran theologian Paul Tillich (1886–1965), who developed his own method of correlation and employed it effectively in his preaching. Reacting against the scholastic theology dominant in the Catholic world in the first part of the twentieth century, Rahner developed a new theological paradigm that brings the Christian message into dialogue with modern thought. His theology begins with a penetrating analysis of human beings as interdependent social creatures who are positively oriented to mystery. We have infinite longings for love and knowledge but find ourselves limited by our finite existence in the world. We ask questions without being able to come up with final compelling answers. Our search for a love that is complete and imperishable remains frustrated as we walk this earth. The real goal of our longings is the holy Mystery, the God beyond all imagining. This Mystery is self-communicating love. The divine outpouring of love creates the whole world, including human beings, who can respond in a personal way. The high point of God's self-giving and human receptivity is found in Jesus Christ, the parable of the Father and the paradigm of fulfilled humanity. Christ reveals the full depths of human existence—that we are fundamentally open to personal union with God. The church is a sacramental communion that proclaims the wisdom of Christ as the best guide for effective human living.

Rahner's theology gains much of its energy from a dialectical tension between the gospel and human experience. The outer word of preaching illumines and judges the inner word of conscience. The Christian message directs our questioning and sheds light on our search for truth. Rahner's theology correlates the

Christian tradition and our historically and culturally conditioned experience, which is always a mixture of grace and sin. Both sides contribute to the exchange and can learn from the other, but Christianity always remains the final judge.

Preaching that is correlational and sacramental gives an important role to God's immanence and to the divine transcendence. Since everything in our graced world is potentially revelatory, homilists can make use of insights from a variety of sources: the personal and collective experience of the congregation; disciplines such as philosophy, psychology, and sociology; contemporary culture with its various art forms; and the world's great religious traditions. This approach takes seriously the context of the Scripture readings: their historical setting and original purpose as well as their significance in the developing tradition of the church. It keeps in mind that the Scriptures are written from multiple perspectives and contain diverse theologies. A correlational homily attempts to link the teaching of the Scripture passages with the explicit concerns of the congregation. In this engagement, the preacher makes clear that the biblical material stands in judgment on contemporary experience and culture.

Liberation theology, including its Latino, Asian, black, and feminist versions, insists that preaching consider the political, economic, and social situation of the hearers of the Word. It is important to recognize and fight against social sin and the false consciousness it engenders. As preachers we must take seriously the experience of those who are oppressed by unjust institutions and live on the margins of society. Effective preaching focuses on the liberation aspects of the biblical message with its call for justice and special care for those in need.

Sacramental preaching is designed to tap human experience and to respond to the real needs and concerns of the congregation; the fundamental danger for this approach is to allow experience to dominate the conversation. This happens when preachers neglect the formative role of the Christian tradition and accept uncritically human experience and cultural patterns, which are always a mixture of grace and sin.

Some preachers may clearly identify with either the dialectical or sacramental approach, while others may find themselves moving between them, depending on circumstances. Whatever the case, it is helpful to reflect on our practice in the light of these two major models so that we can identify our method, build on its strengths, and guard against its weaknesses.

Identifying Our Theology

We can also gain a better understanding of the theology implicit in our preaching by asking how we typically treat the various aspects of the divine–human relationship. Do I tend to stress the graced or sinful aspect of human existence? Is my implied anthropology more individualistic or communal? Do I consciously consider differences between the experience of men and women? Do I take into consideration the social, political, and economic situation of the congregation? What images of God appear most frequently in my homilies? Do I stress more divine mercy or divine judgment? Does my preaching imply that grace is rare and exclusive or abundant and inclusive? Do I tend to present revelation as salvation history, church doctrine, inner illumination, transforming consciousness, or symbolic disclosure? Do I put more stress on extraordinary or ordinary experiences of grace? Am I more optimistic or pessimistic, more inclusive or exclusive in presenting the possibility of salvation? What images of Jesus appear frequently or are neglected in my preaching: the hidden Messiah; the Suffering Servant; the new Elijah, Moses, and David; the compassionate one; the Son of God who knows the secrets of the Father; the new Adam; the great liberator; the parable of the Father; the paradigm of fulfilled humanity; the man for others; and the cosmic Lord? Do I put more emphasis on the cross or the resurrection of Jesus? Do I tend to present the church as a hierarchical institution or as an assembly of disciples? Do I treat the Scriptures as the book produced and interpreted by the church or as the Word of God in judgment on the church? Do I treat Scripture passages uncritically or in the light of modern biblical criticism? Do I present the moral demands of the gospel in terms of high ideals or strict laws? How do I relate the love of God, neighbor, and self? Do I speak about sacraments in more personal terms as encounters with the risen Christ or more communally as special ways the church actualizes itself? Do I emphasize personal salvation in heaven or the collective salvation of the whole world? Do I speak more about the immortality of the soul or the resurrection of the body? What image of heaven comes most readily to mind as I prepare to preach?

More Practical Self-examination

Other, more practical questions can also aid our self-understanding as preachers. How much time do I put into preparation each week? Do I include myself under the judgment of the gospel along with the congregation? Am I more positive or negative in assessing our society and culture? Do I use personal stories that reveal myself, or do I speak more objectively? Do I use humor, and how do I link it with the function of the homily?

Reflection on all these questions can sharpen our awareness of how we actually function as homilists and can suggest ways to enrich and expand our preaching. Both professional development and personal growth are crucial to an effective program of remote preparation for preaching.

KEVIN ANDERSON RESPONSE

Personal development is an essential part of honing the only instrument the preacher carries into the pulpit: him- or herself. Our survey data hint that a preacher's personal and spiritual development (or lack thereof) is apparent to listeners and affects their perception of homilies. The item "This preacher seems to have a strong faith and prayer life" is positively correlated with perceptions of homilies. The item "This preacher lacks personal integrity" has a negative correlation to preacher effectiveness ratings (the higher the score on the "lacking integrity" item, the lower the score on preacher effectiveness). The item "This preacher appears to have a poor understanding of the needs of the congregation" also has a negative correlation to listeners' perceptions of preaching effectiveness.

Relational Development

Any Christian, preacher or not, would do well to develop a personal and spiritual growth plan based on Lonergan's six categories for development (physical, emotional, imaginative, intellectual, moral, and religious). At least two areas, however, are missing: relational and sexual development.

To proclaim the Word authentically, preachers need a deep understanding of human relationships and how grace operates in them, even through conflict and crises. Relationships with people in the congregation are also important for the endeavor of preaching, in part because people do not listen intently to a person for whom they do not have a basic feeling of liking or admiration. The item "This preacher is a very likable person" made the top ten predictors of preacher effectiveness. Knowing a listener's response to this one item allows one to predict just over one third of the variability in preacher effectiveness ratings.

Even more basic than relationships with parishioners is a preacher's own experience of love, family, friendship, conflict, heartache, grief, longing, and all the myriad of experiences that come from intimate relationships with other human beings. To know the heart of listeners, preachers must know the world of intimate relationships, and preferably at a deeper and more personal level than having listened to members of the congregation talk about their experience.

Here are some questions that begin to address the kind of relational development that can deepen the experience a minister brings to addressing the relational concerns of listeners:

- How do I experience intimacy with others?
- What has my experience of family life been, and what is it now?
- What do I know of the joys of deep friendship?
- Do I keep distant from close human connection, possibly because of a history of having been hurt by others?
- Am I naturally extroverted or introverted? How does my personality affect my ability to experience connection to others?

- How do I deal with conflict in relationships?
- What are the areas I most need to grow in to create more loving relationships in my life?
- How does my role as community leader enhance or detract from efforts to be close to others?
- What is my experience of losing loved ones or relationships?
- How have I experienced the receiving or giving of forgiveness?

This is only a partial list. As the spiritual leader of a community, a preacher's relationships inside and outside the community are his or her lifeblood of experience that informs the effort to construct the bridge between Scripture and the human condition. A preacher's homilies will be as alive and engaging as is his or her journey to live out the joys and struggles of love in human relationships. Our data support this. The item "This preacher knows the real struggles of life" was among the top ten predictors, able to account by itself for just over one-third of the variability in preacher's effectiveness ratings.

As a psychologist, I am biased about the value of counseling, because I believe that everyone can benefit from an objective party's input on how to live more effectively. Therefore I encourage preachers, as the spiritual leaders of their communities, to attend to the health of their emotions, thought processes, and relationships, which could include counseling and spiritual direction. Yes, our ministers have schedules as hectic as the lives of the people they serve. Yet that is part of the leadership we need—countercultural models of how to place adequate priority on giving time to personal and spiritual development. A genuine personal growth process cannot be sustained on tidbits of time in a frenetic, work-dominated schedule. Taking time for counseling and spiritual direction is a form of leadership.

Sexual Development

Some may feel that sexual development has little to do with a preacher's role. I disagree. Sexuality is not primarily about whether or how often a person has sex, though many of the people in the pews are very confused about how to integrate their sexuality into a good life. The main reason that sexual development is an important part of what Jim calls remote preparation, however, is that every preacher is either female or male. Sexuality encompasses all of how we interpret being male or female. When sexuality is healthy, life energy flows freely; when it is stymied, shut off, or covered in guilt or shame, life energy is more likely to stagnate, and this lack of vital energy will be felt in all of one's ministerial endeavors, including preaching.

Questions that can help clarify the importance of sexual development for preachers include:

- What is my experience of human affection?
- How have sexual scandals affected how I express my maleness or femaleness with people in the congregation?
- What is my experience of sexuality as depicted in the broader culture?
- Can I articulate a spirituality of sexuality that incorporates moral guidelines and includes a sense of the sacredness of sexual activity?
- Am I familiar with the sexual struggles that many people experience as they attempt to incorporate this mysterious force into their lives?
- Do I strive to integrate both masculine and feminine in my personal growth?
- Do I have a deep knowledge of both male and female experience to inform my preaching to the women and men of my congregation?
- Do I feel free to preach on sexual matters? Is my freedom or lack of freedom in this regard related to how my family of origin talked about or did not talk about sexuality?
- What are the common conflicts between men and women in personal relationships or in the workplace?

Again, these are only sample questions. My point is that sexuality is an inherent part of the human experience about which the secular culture "preaches" incessantly. Those who make up a congregation need mature spiritual guidance in this part of life, which can come from preachers who are actively working on their own sexual development. A mature and growing sense of sexuality will bring deeper understanding and greater vitality to all of a preacher's homilies, not just the few that might deal with sexuality. Great artists often talk about sexuality as a vital force that drives the creative process. If preaching is an art and a craft, it too will flourish best if connected to the great God-given life force of sexuality. Sexuality is such a deeply embedded aspect of the human experience that knowing the heart of listeners requires a keen awareness of one's own experience as a male or female in the world.

Expertness

Implicit in Jim's reflections on remote preparation for preaching is the concept of expertness. If I am going to have heart surgery, I hope that the surgeon has done extensive remote preparation. I would not be comforted, for instance, if the physician said, "Well, I haven't kept up with the journals for ten years or so, but I'll give it my best shot." We need preachers who are experts in spirituality, Scripture, theology, and human experience. If parishioners sense that a preacher isn't expert, the probability of listener shutdown is quite high. Being an expert requires a professional's attitude and the commitment of significant time and energy to personal development and to the preaching ministry.

The only item in our survey that attempted to measure perceived expertness directly was "This preacher is a well-trained expert in Scripture." In the three samples that measured it, this item was positively correlated with overall ratings of preacher effectiveness. Across these samples, about 15 percent of variance in preacher effectiveness scores could be predicted by ratings of a preacher's expertness in Scripture. It is possible that this item did not emerge as one of the stronger predictors, because preachers who come across too much as experts in Scripture may be less mindful of making sure they relate the Scriptures to a real-life existential human concern. As Jim says, if the homily is too far "up there" or "back there" the listener will tune out. Further research would be necessary to study the hypothesis that high levels of expertness in Scripture may attract some listeners and cause others to tune out.

Professional Development

Jim's approach to professional development emphasized awareness of one's implicit or explicit theology that informs the preaching endeavor. This is undoubtedly important, but I think of professional development differently. I would guess that knowing a lot about the game of golf has only moderate correlation to whether a person is a one or a twenty handicap. What produces better scores is lots of practice and feedback from people who know how to play the game well. I think it is time for preachers to "raise their game" by building in a feedback loop designed to improve their preaching continually. It was apparent in reviewing listeners' written comments on over two thousand surveys that some preachers have blind spots that consistently decrease the quality of their preaching. It was striking how a few preachers had many similar negative comments ("Can't hear him" or "Speaks in a monotone" or "Says the same thing every week" or "Talks way too long").

One way to create a feedback loop might be to meet regularly with members of one's congregation to get input on the last homily and gather ideas about what the focus of the homily for the next week should be. The problem with this idea is that it would likely be difficult to find parishioners with the time, communication skills, and willingness to be straightforward in both an affirming and gently challenging way that would be useful to a preacher's development. More helpful, perhaps, would be a regular meeting with a group of peers to review each other's work on videotape and provide encouragement and constructive challenge. A greater realization of and commitment to the importance of preaching could lead faith communities (dioceses, denominations, provinces) to support professional trainers to provide ongoing expert coaching to those who preach the Word.

Theology

While a preacher's awareness of his or her guiding theology is important, an awareness of the theology of the *listeners* is perhaps even more key to whether or not a preacher will be effective. Laypeople are not trained in theology, but each has an implicit theology that guides how she or he thinks about God and the spiritual life. An awareness of listeners' implicit theologies can help preachers craft homilies that will connect with listeners' hearts. Such awareness can also serve as a reminder that listeners need— and most would welcome—a more sophisticated knowledge of the role of diverse theologies in understanding both Scripture and human experience. New theologies open up new possibilities for experiencing a dynamic relationship with God and Scripture.

Our preaching data indicate that similarity between the preacher's and the listener's ideas is an important predictor of the perception of the homily. The item "This preacher usually presents ideas in the sermon very similar to my own" was a top ten predictor of preacher effectiveness scores, accounting by itself for close to 40 percent of the variability of scores. The more similar a listener feels the preacher's ideas are to her or his own, the higher the rating of the preacher tends to be. This is consistent with persuasion theory. Listeners prefer messages that feel "consonant" to those that feel "dissonant" (at odds with one's existing ideas). However, change in a listener's attitudes or behaviors is most likely when there is a moderate discrepancy between a communicator's message and the listener's prior opinion. This makes sense, because it is difficult to produce change when communicator and listener are already in agreement from the start. When a communicator's message diverges too far from the listener's original position (as may occur in prophetic preaching), the probability that the listener will tune the message out completely is much higher.

Preachers who ignore the implicit dominant theology of listeners may make the mistake that many married people make.

Often spouses try to give love in a "love language" that is familiar to them, unaware that their partners actually speak a very different love language. For instance, a husband who tries to give love primarily in a sexual way will experience tension with a wife who primarily wants to receive love through acts of helping around the house or opening up emotionally. Such marriages can go years with a fundamental sense of disconnect. Likewise, preachers who speak one theological language without regard for the dominant theological language of the listeners will not consistently connect effectively with the congregation.

JAMES BACIK RESPONSE

In general, Kevin's comments highlight for me the value of dialogue with the world of psychology. I look to psychology not to provide an overarching framework for preaching, but for specific insights for improving the preaching ministry. Kevin's point that preachers cannot know the hearts of the listeners without an experiential appreciation of personal relationships seems especially important. I was also struck by his suggestion that healthy sexuality allows life energy to flow freely, while guilt and shame are enervating. If preachers bought into Kevin's comparison with the preparation and expertise expected of surgeons, homilies would improve dramatically. In this chapter, Kevin and I combined to pose over forty questions on theology, relationships, and sexuality. Although each of these questions can prompt beneficial personal reflection, they can appear in the aggregate to be overwhelming. Perhaps we who know the challenge of preaching could begin by asking ourselves one simple question: What steps could I take to prepare myself to proclaim the Word more effectively?

CHAPTER THREE

Knowing Your Congregation

To be effective preachers demands that we understand our congregations. Preachers who hope to make the Word credible and meaningful need to know the minds and hearts of their people. We need an appreciation of the dreams that inspire them, the joys that delight them, the sorrows that sadden them, and the demons that assail them. When people sense that the preacher understands their hearts, they are more likely to assimilate the Scripture message.

Knowing through Service and Experience

Pastors of congregations come to know their people through a life of dedicated service: by visiting the sick, counseling the distraught, comforting the bereaved, teaching the searchers. Celebrating baptisms, weddings, and funerals brings us into people's lives at crucial moments. In order to make the most of these opportunities, we need to listen well to our people, attentive to the way they speak about their successes and failures, their loves and fears. It is important to hear behind the words, to discern the deeper convictions and challenges that shape their quest for meaning and purpose. Individuals who appreciate our acts of service are more likely to reveal to us their deepest thoughts and feelings. Over thirty years ago, the Protestant ecclesiologist J. C. Hoekindijk made a comment that has stuck with me: "Proclaiming the name of Jesus should be a P.S. at the end of a long letter of service." We preach more effectively after we have washed feet. Hoekindijk went so far as to say that we should not preach to a congregation we have not served. This advice is not always practical, but it does highlight the essential connection between pastoral ministry and effective preaching.

Our own experience is an important key for interpreting the deeper experiences of our people. Preachers are, first of all, members of the faith community sharing in the universal priesthood of all the baptized disciples of Christ. Like members of our congregation, we stand under the judgment of the gospel. We are all children of the Father, members of Christ's body, and temples of the Holy Spirit. We can relate to our people because their joys and sorrows resonate in our own hearts. Our own practice of prayerful reflection prepares us to discern the deeper dimension of the common experiences shared by our people. A pastor who participates in small faith-sharing groups has a great opportunity to learn how people express their convictions and challenges. In various ways, our experience as pastors enables us to develop a better understanding of the people we serve.

A homilist can also learn more about his or her congregation from the work of scholars. Philosophers describe universal structures that characterize human existence. Psychologists probe the inner workings of the mind. Sociologists help us understand the influence of social institutions and cultural patterns. Historians place current experience in a larger framework of development. Theologians analyze the way biblical wisdom interacts with cultural values in the hearts of people today.

Knowing Human Nature

In the broadest terms, hearers of the Word possess certain universal characteristics or general structures. One way of organizing these general characteristics is in terms of the common search for integration in the midst of the tensions of life. Thus we are all unique individuals with a distinctive face who can fulfill our potential only in various personal communities, especially the family. We are spiritual beings with a taste for the infinite, who remain bound by our bodiliness and the world of time and space.

We are knowers with a drive to understand and explore, who achieve a deeper knowledge only through a life of love. We have the power to shape ourselves and our future, but only under the influence of our past history and previous decisions. We can take hold of ourselves and become our true selves, but only by going outside ourselves and reaching out to other people and the world around us. We are unified whole persons who are continually threatened by self-alienation and disintegrating decisions. In summary, we are self-transcendent, spiritual persons with infinite longings who remain immersed in a world limited by time, space, past history, and our own bodiliness.

In the midst of these essential tensions, human beings continue to search for their identity, fall in love, and grieve the loss of family and friends. Despite our differences, we share in a common search for meaning and purpose in life. Preachers who have a feel for the general human condition and the common human adventure have a better chance of speaking a meaningful word to the congregation.

Premodern Influences

Hearers of the Word today are a product of influences from the premodern, modern, and postmodern eras. Elements of the premodern or medieval world survive primarily in the explicitly religious realm. For example, many people are still unacquainted with modern biblical criticism. They know nothing, for example, about the distinctive literary form of Genesis 1–11; the sources of the Pentateuch; the composition of the gospels; and the intentions of the author of the Book of Revelation. Others are familiar with the broad lines of the historical-critical method but reject it in favor of a premodern mode of interpreting Scripture. Many Christians today maintain a simple premodern understanding of theology that presumes Christian faith is timeless. They have little sense of the development of doctrine, historical disputes, and various schools of contemporary thought. They tend to prefer familiar styles of worship, assuming that the church has always done it that way.

Modern Influences

The various components of the modern world continue to influence the consciousness of Christians today. These include the *Enlightenment*, with its optimistic confidence in the power of reason and the accomplishments of science to further human progress; *Romanticism*, with its positive notions of human nature and its celebration of human creativity; *patriarchy*, with its insistence on male superiority in the public realm and women's responsibility for domestic affairs; *colonialism*, with its assumption of the superiority of Western culture; *denominationalism*, with its acceptance of divisions among Christians and stereotypical views of other believers; the *book culture*, with its linear thinking and analytic mode of consciousness; the *spirit of exploration*, with its desire to extend human knowledge and control. All of these factors that created modernity are still alive in the collective consciousness of Americans and can be found in varying degrees in the minds and hearts of individuals.

Modernity today is influenced by enduring Romantic criticisms of the Enlightenment project. Rationalism fragments human life by splitting reason and feeling and by separating us from nature. Industrialization has harmed the natural environment and produced widespread pollution. Rugged individualism undermines concern for the common good and weakens participatory democracy. Bureaucratic structures depersonalize human existence. Enlightenment ideals of universal justice, equality, freedom, democracy, and the limitation of suffering are in danger of collapsing without the firm foundation of religious beliefs and practices. The fundamental tension of modernity between the Enlightenment celebration of reason and the Romantic emphasis on creative imagination is still found in modern church members who struggle to integrate head and heart, reason and emotion, human progress and respect for nature, individual freedom and the common good, efficiency and respect for persons, secular ideals and religious convictions.

We are indeed living in an age of transition as we move into the postmodern world, but the ethos of the modern world continues to exercise great influence. Modern believers are generally open to preaching that reinterprets and refocuses the Christian message in a contemporary context, showing how the gospel illumines and guides the human adventure.

Postmodern Influences and Challenges

Elements of the postmodern mentality are making an increasingly greater impact on the contemporary consciousness. Important events have challenged and disrupted the fundamental optimism of modernity: the *World Wars*, which defied reason and turned technological advances into weapons of mass destruction; *industrialization*, which dehumanized labor and produced widespread pollution; the *Great Depression and other economic fluctuations*, which demonstrated the limitations of economic planning; *totalitarian regimes*, which turned utopian dreams into repressive nightmares; the *assassination of President John F. Kennedy*, which introduced chaos into Camelot; *terrorist attacks*, especially September 11, 2001, which have produced a radical sense of vulnerability; *technological tragedies*, including the Challenger and Columbia, which remind us of the limitations of science.

Persistent social problems also threaten to erode the confidence of American citizens. The great moral issue of abortion still divides the country, and we have not yet found an acceptable way to frame the question so that we can have a civil argument about it. Racial tensions persist, and affirmative action polarizes public opinion. Interest groups subvert the political process while pushing their own agenda. Parents worry about their children, contending with a youth subculture that promotes drugs and sexual promiscuity. The high divorce rate disrupts family life and hurts children. Corporate downsizing and plant closings suddenly thrust hardworking individuals into the ranks of the unemployed. The debate over the war against Iraq brought protesters into the streets.

Congregations bombarded by so many painful events and social ills can easily develop a collective amnesia and forget the amazing positive developments of recent decades: the collapse of the Soviet Union and the end of the Cold War; the liberation of Eastern Europe, which gave new freedom to millions; the freeing of Nelson Mandela and his service as president of South Africa; the destruction of the Berlin Wall and the reunification of Germany; growing economic freedom in China. These events, with their admitted ambiguities and limitations, represent unprecedented progress toward greater freedom for millions of people. And yet these truly remarkable developments do not seem to have much of an impact on ordinary American citizens. It is as though the constant bombardment of negative stories and images blunts our ability to appreciate the positive and savor the triumphs.

Postmodern Tasks

Hearers of the Word today are drawn into the great task of constructing the postmodern world. Many people are trying to determine how to relate as male and female on the basis of respect and mutuality while moving beyond modern patriarchy, which diminishes both sexes. Citizens have a responsibility to join the national debate on how the United States, as the lone superpower, can be a force for good in the world while avoiding the arrogance of modern colonialism. Christians have the opportunity to forge a new unity among the followers of Jesus that overcomes the divisions of modern denominationalism. People have to make a living and contribute to the common good in a postindustrial society. We all must learn to live in the electronic world of television and the Internet, utilizing their enormous power to shrink the globe and provide information while overcoming their tendencies to dehumanize life and diminish community. The emerging world is postpatriarchal, postcolonial, postdenominational, postindustrial, and post–Cold War. The precise shape of this postmodern world, apart from its electronic character, is not clear. Hearers of the Word are not only influenced by these developments but face the challenge of living in one of the great transitional periods in the history of the world with all of its disruptions and discontinuities.

The Problem of Relativism

A culture in such great flux challenges traditional certainties and fosters a spirit of relativism. Today a growing number of people resonate with the prediction of the nineteenth-century philosopher Friedrich Nietzsche that with the collapse of absolute truth, represented by the death of God, people would "feel the breath of empty space" while straying through "an infinite nothing" unable to determine up from down. Contemporary deconstructionist scholars feed this relativism by denying various claims to absolute truth: the Christian claim to a universal message of salvation, the philosophical claim to a comprehensive explanation of reality, literary claims to a normative reading of classic texts, religious claims to an overreaching story or meganarrative valid for every culture, and church claims to interpret the Bible in an official way. Most parishioners do not encounter deconstructionist thought directly, but they do live in a culture rife with relativism that affects the consciousness of individuals in subtle ways.

The Influence of the Electronic Media

Our parishioners are more directly influenced by the postmodern electronic modes of communication. As the invention of the printing press created a book culture and a linear form of consciousness, so television and the Internet are producing a new form of consciousness that is more symbolic, holistic, receptive, intuitive, and simultaneous. Television bombards individuals with images that enter consciousness without much chance for analysis, and the Internet supplies vast amounts of information without an interpretive key for organizing or understanding it. The electronic culture makes it difficult to achieve a comprehensive view of reality and to develop a reflective and centered sense of interiority. In the postmodern electronic world, time and space are compressed. We communicate easily with people around the globe. Billions of people watch popular events like the Olympic Games at the same time. The generations who grew up watching television and using computers are at ease in this world and reflect the strengths and weaknesses of the electronic culture. But even previous generations, who were formed by the book culture, cannot escape the pervasive influence of the electronic modes of communication that shape our consciousness.

The Distinctive American Experience

Hearers of the Word in the United States are still influenced by the great movements of the past that have shaped the ethos of our country. The early Puritan dream of establishing a new world through discipline and hard work has survived in the religious commitment to spread the kingdom and the secular pursuit of the American dream. Many citizens do not share in the American dream, including those caught in the hellish circle of poverty and those suffering from discrimination. Some have become cynical about the connection between hard work and achieving success. They do not trust that the institutions of society will reward them for honest effort.

The political insights of our founding fathers, well represented by Thomas Jefferson, remain deeply rooted in the American psyche. Our political revolution in the late eighteenth century was not antireligious or anticlerical, like the French Revolution. Our country did not have a premodern history that demanded revision. Jefferson and most of his colleagues did not espouse atheism or regard the church as an obstacle to human progress—on the contrary, they expressed belief in a Creator who wrote the divine law into nature and endowed us with certain inalienable rights. They saw religion as playing a positive role in the ordering of human life, and they adopted the First Amendment to create a framework for religious peace. This amendment, while preventing the establishment of any religion, ensures that citizens can practice their own religion without coercion and with complete freedom. Under this arrangement, religion has flourished in the United States. We are, as the Supreme Court said, a religious people. Our parishioners are part of the large majority—over 90 percent—who believe in God and who pray regularly. Most of our people are comfortable with the non-establishment clause of the First Amendment and treasure the religious freedom we enjoy.

Our political arrangement fosters tolerance and allows for widespread belief, but it does not ensure depth of religious commitment. Some studies suggest that less than 20 percent of believers in the United States are fully committed to their religious tradition and try to live it on a daily basis in all phases of life. As finite human beings, we all know the gap between ideals and actual practice. No Christian can completely live up to the demands of discipleship.

The American Civil Religion

In the United States, this problem is more complex because many nominal Christians actually hold and practice a different set of beliefs and values, which the sociologist Robert Bellah has described as the American civil religion. The fundamental myth of this religious symbol system is modeled on the exodus—an oppressed people escaped from the tyrants in Europe, crossed a body of water, and settled in a new promised land. These immigrants thought of themselves as a chosen people destined to be a light to other nations. At its best the civil religion highlights the sovereignty of God, who is the source of all human rights and the judge of human actions. The American civil religion functions as a symbol system with saints (Washington and Jefferson), holy days (Thanksgiving and Memorial Day), sacred writings (the Declaration of Independence and the Constitution), and special symbols (the Flag and Great Seal), but it says little about Jesus. He is usually not even mentioned, for example, in the official lighting of the national Christmas tree.

Although scholars dispute specifics of Bellah's analysis, there is no doubt that some form of American idealism affects the consciousness of citizens today. The key question is how the American dream relates to Christian faith. Do people think of themselves first of all as Americans who happen to be Christian, or as Christians who happen to live in the United States? Some, no doubt, pledge allegiance first to the flag and then to the cross. When the gospel and national interests seem to be in conflict, they opt for nationalism. Others seem to vacillate, depending on the issue, between allegiance to cross or to flag. Crises of national security seem to surface more Christian Americans. This analysis accounts for much of the religious tension among church members and presents a great challenge to preachers.

Individualism

Churchgoers are also influenced by the individualism that is such a powerful force in American life. Utilitarian individualism, which gained influence throughout the nineteenth and twentieth centuries, is manifest in economics as the pursuit of personal gain without regard for others; in politics as a selfish accumulation of power; in family life as an unwillingness to sacrifice; in religion as a preoccupation with personal salvation. Today we also see a more expressive type of individualism that strongly emphasizes personal fulfillment in the emotional, imaginative, and intellectual areas of life without sufficient concern for the welfare of others. In its extreme forms, individualism celebrates the rights and opportunities of individuals to the detriment of the common good. Our culture also manifests a significant countertrend that values genuine public service, sacrifice for the sake of others, dedication to family life, and commitment to extending the reign of justice and peace in the world. Hearers of the Word today know the struggle among the various forms of individualism and genuine commitment to the common good.

Consumerism

It is difficult to live in the United States without being influenced by consumerism. The world of advertising bombards us with clever messages that certain products are necessary for happiness, comfort, and status. This contributes to the unexamined assumption that having is more important than being, and that personal worth is measured more by possessions than by character. Consumerism helps create a great deal of dissatisfaction among those who cannot afford the luxuries associated with the good life. It turns human goods, such as love and respect, into commodities and creates the illusion that they can be purchased or acquired on demand. Our affluent society, driven by acquisitive desires, has produced a greater interest in a simple lifestyle. According to some recent polls, most Americans now place a

higher priority on improving personal relationships than on raising their standard of living. A growing number of employees are
trying to build their careers around their family commitments by
working at home or developing more flexible work schedules.
Some people purposely seek simpler leisure activities that are less
expensive and more nourishing for the spirit.

Church members in the United States reflect the tensions
built into American culture, between Christianity and civil religion, consumerism and a simpler lifestyle, individualism and the
common good. Individuals have their distinctive ways of relating
to the dominant culture and the countertrends. Some simply buy
into the dominant culture without considering the challenge of
the gospel. Others stand resolutely against questionable cultural
values on the basis of their Christian faith. In between these
extremes, we find many constructive approaches: for example,
adopting a simple lifestyle in imitation of Jesus; seeking a communal form of self-fulfillment in accord with the gospel; accepting the sovereignty of God espoused by civil religion, while seeing
Christ as the primary revelation of the divine will. The variations
are multiple, and it is difficult to develop adequate models. It is
important, however, to remember that contemporary hearers of
the Word must wrestle with difficult cultural tensions.

Generational Differences

Preachers should also keep in mind the generational differences found in our congregations. The conclusions of sociologists
who study generational cohorts often filter down to us in a popular form. Cohorts manifest certain characteristics in response to
major events. Those who lived through the Great Depression and
World War II tend to be persevering, gritty, and frugal with a
strong sense of hard work, sacrifice, and personal responsibility.
According to the popular image, baby boomers, who came of age
during the rebellious sixties and the "me decade" of the seventies,
were more interested in pursuing the good life of economic pros-
perity and personal freedom and are now reconsidering their values and priorities. The more recent generations, commonly called

Generation X and the millennials, have known great disruptions and discontinuities in their lives: family breakups; governmental corruption; church polarization; corporate scandals; space shuttle tragedies; the AIDS epidemic; and terrorist attacks, especially on September 11, 2001. As a result, young people often experience a tension between their natural optimism and the sober realities of life at the beginning of the new century. Most collegians, for example, are doubtful about the health of the nation's economy, but remain confident that they themselves will do well financially. Those who come from broken homes tend to be more cautious about entering marriage, but still believe they can make it work. A surprising number of collegians feel close to their parents, even though they often resent the excesses and failures of the previous generation. In the midst of a great deal of political apathy, about one-third of freshmen students enrolling in four-year colleges believe that following politics is a very important goal. Collegians, who generally manifest very little enduring loyalty to a particular religious denomination, are showing an increased interest in spirituality and the distinctive traits of their received traditions. Young people have the task of appropriating their received faith so it can serve as a source of overarching meaning and a solid guide for their lives. In trying to make their received traditions their own, they often pass through periods of doubt and need guidance in coming to a more mature faith that relates them to God and others in healthy ways. Some young people accomplish this task by reinterpreting the Christian message and adapting to the culture; others are more concerned with preserving the traditions and finding a clear religious identity.

My own experience with Catholic collegians over the last three decades suggests that students today are on a spiritual journey very similar to that of their parents. With previous generations they share the same spiritual longings for meaning and purpose in life. These millennials, as they are sometimes called, have to contend with the essential conflict between their infinite longings and their finite capabilities. They know the age-old struggle between grace and sin. Their challenges sound familiar: forming their personal identity, developing good friendships, finding a life partner, choosing a career, appropriating their religious heritage, cultivating habits of good citizenship, and deciding how to relate to the dominant culture. Fads in music, dress, dance, and language change rapidly, while human nature remains common. Millennials still fall in love, treasure friends, and empathize with suffering loved ones.

American culture continues to exercise great influence on millennial collegians, often at a preconscious level. Some cultural trends, such as rugged individualism, unbridled hedonism, lavish consumerism, and uncritical nationalism are anti-gospel and harmful to their spiritual growth. Other ideals, including authenticity, self-actualization, freedom, and volunteerism, when placed in a Christian framework, can promote healthy spiritual development. Collegians grow up in a country in which over 90 percent of the citizens say they believe in God and pray periodically, and over 60 percent are affiliated with a religious organization. During the last four years of the twentieth century, polls indicated that interest in spirituality among teenagers increased almost 25 percent, a trend that anecdotal evidence suggests is continuing. Collegians reflect the ambivalent mix of secular and religious currents in our culture.

For the most part, the richly textured Catholic subculture that shaped Catholic spirituality in the past has disappeared. Catholic millennials have grown up with greater religious pluralism than their grandparents. Most of them have not known an integrated Catholic world that transmits a coherent vision of the faith. Rather, they have gleaned fragments of their spirituality from various sources, including their families, parish liturgies, youth retreats, religious education classes, and, for some, Catholic schools. This process has produced collegians with greater tolerance but less institutional loyalty than previous generations of Catholics.

Recent sociological studies of young adults indicate that most Catholic collegians today maintain certain fundamental beliefs that can help ground a viable spirituality. Around 90 percent affirm the divinity of Christ and believe that at Mass the bread and wine become his body and blood. They consider helping the poor to be as important to their faith as believing in the real presence of Christ in the Eucharist. Although most Catholic collegians have no explicit working knowledge of the Second Vatican Council, many have appropriated important conciliar themes, presumably from diverse ecclesial and cultural sources. Foremost is the crucial conviction that we are the church, which, for all practical purposes, means that the faithful should have a voice in how parishes are run. These millennials also demonstrate an incipient understanding of the communal nature of the liturgy, the importance of religious liberty, the value of ecumenical and interfaith dialogue, the expanded role of laity in the church, the unique mediatorship of Christ, and the need to work for social justice. My students often find that formal study of these conciliar teachings affirms general perceptions that they already hold.

Although Catholic millennials share certain common characteristics, their spiritual passions and interests are quite diverse. We can examine this pluralism by distinguishing seven types of spirituality: eclipsed, private, ecumenical, evangelical, sacramental, prophetic, and communal.

(1) *Eclipsed.* A good number of Catholic collegians show no particular interest in religious or spiritual matters. They do not attend Mass on campus and seldom pray. Some feel they are too busy or have higher priorities, while others experience guilt feelings that blunt their spiritual longings. Yet they remain religious beings and identify themselves as Catholics in surveys. Their spirituality is not destroyed but is, rather, eclipsed by their current concerns. We can hope that the ordinary process of maturation or some major events, such as a personal crisis, the death of a loved one, getting married, or having a baby, will uncover their latent spiritual needs.

(2) *Private.* Some Catholic collegians seldom attend liturgies or participate in church activities but pursue spiritual goals in other ways—for example, reading religious books, communing with nature, and praying privately. Their private spiritual journey can be fulfilling but, unconnected to traditional wisdom, it is threatened by fads and superficiality. Our hope is that they will discover and tap the rich spiritual tradition of their Catholic heritage.

(3) *Ecumenical.* A growing number of millennials simply assume that the divisions among Christians make no sense and that we all should unite and work together. Some are loyal to their Catholic heritage, but others have little institutional loyalty and would join another Christian denomination if it brought them closer to Christ and better served their spiritual needs. In this

competitive situation, we need vibrant Catholic parishes that will utilize the gifts of today's collegians and meet their needs.

(4) *Evangelical.* A small percentage of Catholic collegians manifests a piety that resembles the evangelical Christian groups on campus. They speak easily about their personal relationship to Jesus and gravitate to prayer groups with high emotional energy. Some are charismatic in orientation, emphasizing the gifts of the Holy Spirit. A few are really fundamentalists who act aggressively in preserving their Catholic heritage from the threats of the contemporary world and the reforms of Vatican II, which appear to them as excessive and dangerous. The church on campus should make room for the evangelical Catholics and learn how to tap their energy and enthusiasm.

(5) *Sacramental.* Many Catholic millennials still love their church and find their spiritual nourishment through fairly regular participation in the official liturgy and traditional practices. As a result, they are attuned to the presence of God in everyday life and have a general sense of the sacramental character of the whole world. Some of them report mystical experiences, while others simply trust that God is present in their daily lives. These students often need affirmation that their spiritual intuitions accord with the core spirituality of the Catholic tradition.

(6) *Prophetic.* Most campus ministry programs have a small group of students committed to working in various ways for justice and peace in the world. They align themselves with the goals of organizations like Pax Christi and Bread for the World, devote themselves to causes such as racial harmony and environmental health, and try to help those in need. The developing tradition of Catholic social thought can be a great source of guidance and inspiration for them.

(7) *Communal.* Many millennial Catholics feel the need to associate with others who share their values. They like worshiping with kindred spirits at Mass, using their gifts for the benefit of the church, and participating in faith-sharing groups. They often need reminders that an authentic communal spirituality maintains dialogue with the larger world.

The older categories of conservative and liberal, based on responses to Vatican II, are no longer adequate to describe the

Catholic millennials, who have no experience and little knowledge of the council. They have a new set of challenges and diverse ways of relating to the Catholic tradition, but they are empowered by the same Spirit, who is the real basis of our hope for this generation of collegians.

Preachers face a great challenge in constructing homilies that address the needs and interests of young and old as well as the differences within generational cohorts. Given the great religious and cultural pluralism in the United States, it is not possible to develop a clear typology that adequately illumines the differences in the average congregation. Pastors can prepare more effective homilies, however, by listening well to their people, conscious of the typical tensions between faith and culture prevalent today.

KEVIN ANDERSON RESPONSE

Jim's analysis of the many cultural factors that shape both preacher and listener is important because it is so easy for the gospel and those who preach it to become completely acculturated. When this happens, the gospel loses its power to challenge the culture, and preachers lose their power to call listeners to something beyond a secular worldview that coexists too easily with a compartmentalized understanding of religion and worship. The "isms" that Jim discusses have relevance not just for the prophetic possibilities of preaching. People need help recognizing that their daily lives are saturated with grace, that God is immanent, not distant—an awareness that is easily lost when we allow culture to be the primary determinant of our worldview.

Micro and Macro

There are two levels of "knowing the congregation"—the micro level, which has to do with the details and lived experience of daily life, and the macro level, which concerns analysis of the larger forces that shape the consciousness and worldview of those who attend church. Jim's comments seem to be addressed primarily to the macro level. As experts, preachers need to know about such things as premodern influences and postmodern relativism, but the most basic form of knowing the congregation must go deeper than the macro. It must go deeper even than the experience of being with and serving others as they experience the ups and downs of life. It begins with awareness of one's own experience of being human.

As Jim has said, listeners want preachers who are familiar with and have wrestled with the great questions. This is supported by our data. The item "This preacher knows the real struggles of life" is correlated positively with preacher ratings and is a top ten predictor. Some of these great life questions are influenced by social forces—generationalism, consumerism, relativism, and so on—but they are encountered most directly in the daily decisions, experiences, and activities of people.

Our studies of preaching effectiveness found that the item "This preacher's sermons make me feel like he or she knows what is in my heart" is highly correlated with a homily's effectiveness. Across our three largest samples, this predictor was second only to "This preacher's style of delivering the sermon helps keep my attention." Listeners won't get the "knows what is in my heart" feeling from a description of social forces alone. What is needed is the ability to communicate how those forces impact our individual lives—our relationships, our time, our longings, our small and large decisions. A preacher who can communicate a genuine sense of having wrestled with the difficulty of keeping spiritually centered in a materialistic, work-centered, time-starved culture will have listeners' full attention. When he preaches, Jim is unusually effective at telling stories about real people (with details disguised to protect confidence) to bring to awareness the universal human concerns that he wishes to address.

I think preaching books would be more widely read and studied if the "micro" aspect of knowing the congregation were the starting point. Consumerism, for instance, is a label we place on a human phenomenon that we experience in daily life as the desire to acquire more and more things. What is the preacher's experience of this powerful force? How has he or she experienced others struggling with it? How do we reconcile living in such a culture with gospel values? From a "micro" point of view, then,

understanding the congregation involves being intimately familiar with the joys, struggles, and longings of the human heart.

What Is in Listeners' Hearts?

What are some of these great questions that people carry in
their hearts?

- Who am I? What am I meant to do with my life?
- How can I experience deep, loving relationships?
- What should I do for meaningful work in the world?
- How do I support my family financially, yet not make
  money too important?
- How do I create a beautiful marriage?
- How do I raise my children in the best manner possible?
- Why do evil and suffering exist?
- How do I handle conflict, forgiveness, failure, sin, and
  other shadow sides of being human?
- How do I get through life's most difficult crises?
- How do I create a healthy relationship with time?
- Is it wrong to be wealthy or to want to be wealthy?
- How can I celebrate a responsible and enjoyable sexuality?
- What is happiness and how does one find it? Why is it
  often so fleeting?
- Who or what is God?
- How can I be more aware of or connected to God?
- What happens when we die?

Jim will raise many more questions similar to the ones above
when he addresses in chapter 5 the importance of tuning into
human concerns in determining the focus of the homily. To me,
knowing the congregation means probing one's own engagement
with such questions and being aware of how the members of one's
congregation struggle with them. Celibate ministers do not share
a daily lived experience of marriage and family life with their
parishioners, but all human beings wrestle with the great questions, regardless of lifestyle.

Finitude

Jim's emphasis on the contrast of human beings' infinite longings with their finite capabilities is so important. This is a fundamental aspect of human experience that I've rarely heard addressed in homilies. That is probably because to preach about finitude is countercultural. Perhaps even preachers have been drawn into the nonconscious American ideology that life has no limits. People know too well the limits of their own lives, but tend to think that somebody, somewhere, has found a way to put the whole package called "happiness" together. It is so important to let people know that longing, incompleteness, finitude, and imperfection are all essential parts of the spiritual journey.

Prophetic Preaching

Jim will discuss prophetic preaching in chapter 6, but a brief comment is in order here. The culture constantly bombards all seekers with unspiritual influences, the way a boulder in a mountain stream is pounded by a raging torrent following a downpour. The forces that Jim discussed at the "macro" level are not incidental to the spiritual experience—they shape how people think about and live out both daily life and the spiritual journey. Preaching that challenges listeners to be aware of the insidious spiritual effects of the various "isms" is prophetic, countercultural preaching—and it is much needed. Prophetic preaching need not become political (advocating certain causes or candidates from the pulpit). There is plenty of material in the tension between secular culture and gospel values. Parishioners live with this tension, though they may have found ways to reduce the disturbing dissonance it creates. Addressing the dissonance and giving suggestions for how to live more integrated, gospel-inspired lives are at the core of prophetic preaching.

JAMES BACIK RESPONSE

Kevin's helpful distinction between the macro and micro levels prompts a personal reflection. As pastor of a university parish,

I preach regularly to collegians. My bio includes these distinctive descriptors: male celibate priest who came of age in the Eisenhower years and was jolted by the assassination of President Kennedy; sports fan who retains vivid images of watching Ted Williams hit, George Mikan shoot hook shots, and Jimmy Brown break tackles; book reader who organizes material in outlines; listener of classical music who knows little about popular rock groups and wants the amplified music turned down at wedding receptions; watcher of news programs who has never seen most prime-time television programs. My task is to preach to collegians who are preparing for marriage, are still processing September 11th, never heard of George Mikan, think in collages, listen to rock music, watch prime-time television, and want the music turned up louder at social gatherings.

Our survey results and anecdotal evidence support my own sense that I can still do an acceptable job of proclaiming the gospel to these students. For me, the key is listening to them with an open heart and critical mind. When I listen well, I detect common human concerns behind the distinctive details of their stories. As did previous generations, including my own, they celebrate the joys of success, struggle with fears and disappointments, seek self-fulfillment, desire healthy relationships, and battle against dark forces that look awfully familiar. In dealing with collegians for over thirty years, I am more impressed with the commonality of their experiences than with the changing patterns of expression.

Listening to students, I pick up the characteristic ways they speak about the matters that concern them most. I may not know the latest hit song, but I do recognize the cry of the heart for recognition and approval. I may have to ask students to tell me about a popular television program, but I can detect what this reveals about their values and interests. My framework for interpreting what collegians say is shaped by my own experience and my understanding of the tensions prevalent in the world we share.

Every year I teach a credit course on contemporary theology that is essentially a popularized version of Rahner's *Foundations of Christian Faith* (New York: Crossroad, 1982). A good portion of the class time is devoted to discussing a particular personal or social concern, such as how to form healthy relationships or what can be done to promote justice and peace. This is a marvelous opportunity to learn what collegians are thinking and feeling about important issues and to prod them to deeper reflection and more precise articulation of their experience. These discussions sometimes lead to private conversations or counseling sessions with students who invite me to share an important part of their journey. When I succeed in passing over to their viewpoint, I return to my own standpoint more aware of the distinct ways students experience their world and speak about it.

Drawing on my discussions with the students, I often include in my homilies composite stories that are disguised but that still manifest the realism of ordinary conversation about significant issues. These personal stories usually reflect a larger context that takes into account cultural trends and social tensions.

In a recent homily I told the story, based on an informal conversation, of a student who felt burned-out near the end of the semester: sleeping about four hours a night, having trouble staying awake in class, fighting with his girlfriend over trivial matters, and wondering if his life makes any sense. I used the story to exemplify the common problem shared by many, including the homilist, of managing time in our success-oriented culture. This set up a reflection on the image of the the vine and the branches in John 15:1–8, which stresses the need to remain with Christ (for example, through public and private prayer) in order to bear fruit and live more effectively. Thus the homily combined the micro level of the personal experience of the student and the preacher and the macro level of cultural trends that affect us all. Hearers of the Word who recognize this concern are prepared to reflect more deeply on the image of the vine and the branch.

CHAPTER FOUR

Interpreting the Scriptures

After considering our personal development as preachers and delineating general characteristics of those who hear the Word, we turn to the general task of interpreting the Bible. The work of interpreting Scripture is difficult, requiring not only an open heart but also a good deal of background knowledge. We are trying to understand a book that is really a whole library of individual books, written by many different authors over more than a thousand-year period. The worldview, culture, language, and psychology of these authors, who lived at least nineteen hundred years ago, are quite different from our own. Some books, such as Isaiah, contain material from more than one author and reflect changing social and cultural circumstances. Biblical authors used various literary forms, some of which are not immediately familiar to us today. The traditional Christian claim that God is the author of the Bible and that Scripture is the Word of God raises questions about interpretations that appear contradictory or opposed to modern understandings. Even biblical scholars know the temptation to read into Scripture passages their own opinions and worldviews.

Determining the Literal Meaning

As preachers who face the challenge of uncovering the meaning of specific texts, we have valuable resources in the long tradition of biblical interpretation as well as more modern approaches. We should begin our interpretation with a search for the literal meaning of a passage, the sense directly intended by the original author and conveyed by the words of the text. This literal sense is not always the obvious surface meaning of the passage: for example, the six-day creation in Genesis is not a divine truth to be defended against modern evolutionary theory. We do not uncover the literal meaning by detaching a universal truth from a biblical story: for instance, deriving the fidelity of God from the story of Noah and the flood. There is always the danger of assuming that the author's intention matches our own agenda and interests or that the literal meaning is whatever the congregation needs to hear.

More authentic interpretations make use of modern biblical criticism, which is quite accessible through general commentaries, especially the multivolume *Anchor Bible*, edited by David Noel Freedman (New York: Doubleday, 1992), and the one-volume *New Jerome Biblical Commentary*, edited by Raymond E. Brown et al. (Englewood Cliffs, NJ: Prentice-Hall, 1990). The lectionary-based commentaries (for example: *Preaching the Lectionary* by Reginald Fuller [Collegeville, MN: Liturgical Press, 1984]; *Preaching through the Christian Year* by Fred Craddock et al. [Valley Forge, PA: Trinity Press International, 1992–94]; *Footprints on the Mountain* by Roland Faley [New York: Paulist Press, 1994]; and *Preaching the New Lectionary* by Dianne Bergant [Collegeville, MN: Liturgical Press, 1999–2000]) help us determine the historical setting of a given passage, the sociological situation of the audience, and the intent of the author, as well as the literary form used. If we realize that Jonah is a fictional parable, probably written in the fifth century when an intense nationalism was common among the Jews, then we can understand the author's intent to poke fun at religious exclusivism. The commentaries make available to us the scholarly work of the form critics, who trace the development of units of material within books of the Bible, and the insights of redaction critics, who examine, for example, the creative role of the evangelists in editing and shaping the gospel material. The scholars who tell us that the early Christian community added an explanation to the original parable of Jesus about the sower and the seed help us understand the literal meaning intended by the author and found in the gospel text. With all this help from modern scholarship, we can gain a relatively adequate understanding of the literal meaning of most passages in the Bible.

Fuller Senses of Scripture

A preacher must also consider the deeper nonliteral meaning of Scripture texts. Traditionally, Christians have assumed that there is a fuller sense or an implicit meaning in Scripture that goes beyond the explicit intent of an individual author. The preacher often uncovers this deeper meaning and derives connections beyond the author's conscious intention, simply by reading the passage in the context of the entire Bible. We do this when we follow the New Testament practice of understanding passages in the Hebrew Scriptures in the light of their fulfillment in Jesus. Augustine succinctly enunciated the principle: "The New Testament is hidden in the Old and the Old Testament is illumined through the New." Following New Testament practice, preachers often understand persons, places, and events in the past as types that foreshadow the future saving actions of God in the world: for example, Jonah in the whale anticipates the death and resurrection of Jesus. Some preachers tend to make more imaginative allegorical connections, as did Origen and other fathers of the church, who interpreted the bride in the Song of Songs as a foreshadowing of the church as bride of Christ and of the nuptial relationship between our souls and Christ.

An even broader use of Scripture involves using texts to explain or highlight a contemporary event or issue that has no real intrinsic connection: for instance, some preachers lauded Pope John XXIII by citing the passage: "There was a man sent from God whose name was John" (John 1:6). We can also interpret the Scriptures in terms of our own inner life in ways beyond the intention of the author. Thus, we could use the story of the cure of the paralytic (Mark 2:1–12) to discuss ways in which individuals are paralyzed emotionally or spiritually. A homilist who is concerned about justice issues can find passages that support current causes: for instance, arguing against the death penalty on the basis of Luke's portrayal of Jesus as the liberator of captives (4:18).

Contemporary preachers who find various levels of deeper meaning in the Scriptures are following a long Christian tradition. Origen emphasized the spiritual sense for mature Christians, and Augustine made use of allegorical interpretations. Although

Thomas Aquinas emphasized the literal meaning of biblical passages, he recognized a spiritual meaning as well. Martin Luther,
who opposed allegorizing interpretations, still practiced a typo-
logical exegesis that saw Christ in Old Testament passages. All of
these historical precedents free preachers today to discern and use
fuller meanings in biblical texts. At the same time, we must recognize both the importance of uncovering the literal meaning and
the danger of misreading texts by imposing our own meanings on
them and reading our own bias into them. The text cannot defend
itself against ideological interpretations that impose an unin-
tended meaning on them.

Probing the Parables

We can illustrate this search for the meaning of Scripture
passages by examining the parables of Jesus in greater detail. The
parables are familiar fare for Christians: the Good Samaritan, the
Prodigal Son, the Pharisee and the Tax Collector, the Lost Sheep,
the Rich Man and Lazarus, and the many others found in the
Synoptic Gospels. But the parables are difficult to interpret and
do not easily yield their deeper meaning. They are deliberately
enigmatic, designed to challenge common assumptions and to
promote deeper reflection. They reflect a time and a culture that
are foreign to us. It is impossible to extract one precise meaning
from them, because they are open to various legitimate interpretations. Moreover, our very familiarity with the parables makes it
more difficult to derive new insights from them. When we hear
the opening lines of a well-known parable, it is easy to shut down
mentally because we assume that we already know the story and
what it signifies. It takes a conscious effort to derive more from
the parables of Jesus.

As preachers, we have to work hard to hear the parables in a
fresh way, as if we were hearing them for the first time. Specific
strategies can help: be attentive to all the details, determine the main
character in the dramatic stories, speculate on the motivations of the
various characters and try to identify with one of them, imagine
how the unresolved aspects of the story turn out. For example,

concentrate on the older son in the parable of the Prodigal Son, with various questions in mind: How does he relate to his father? Why does he not want to go to the party for his brother? Does he end up going or not? How am I like him? Retelling a parable in our own words can also suggest new interpretations and surprising insights.

Allegorical Interpretations

While we should feel free to make allegorical interpretations of the parables by applying the details of the stories to our current situation, we should do so within the framework of Christian teaching. It is helpful to think of Lazarus as representing poor people in the world today; but it is not legitimate to compare the self-righteous Pharisee to all those who happen to disagree with us. In 1888, Adolf Jülicher published a seminal two-volume work in German that argued that the original parables of Jesus were not allegories and that he did not intend the details of the stories to refer to some future reality. This generally accepted analysis warns us against bizarre and arbitrary applications of the parables.

But the church has always made use of allegorical interpretations. The evangelist Mark offered a detailed allegorical explanation of the parable of the Sower and the Seed by comparing the seed to the Word of the Lord and using the details of the story (for example, seed falling among thorns) to explain why some people reject the teaching of Jesus. In the fifth century, Augustine proposed this allegorical interpretation of the parable of the Good Samaritan: the man who was beaten and robbed is Adam; Jerusalem, from whence he came, is the state of original happiness, while Jericho represents human mortality; the Samaritan is Christ, the inn is the church, and the innkeeper is the apostle Paul. We can get more out of the parables by concentrating on how they illumine our current efforts to be authentic disciples. Allegorical interpretations faithful to the thrust of the Gospel can help.

Discovering the Main Point of the Parable

Some homilists concentrate on extracting from a parable the one major teaching that arises from the primary point of comparison. Thus, in the story of the Prodigal Son the reconciling gesture of the father to his wayward son teaches us that God has unbounded mercy for sinners. This method of interpretation, which was proposed by Jülicher before the turn of the century, was dominant among scholars until the 1960s. Even though scholars have developed new approaches, it remains a helpful way of reading the parables without getting lost in unimportant details or strained comparisons. The parable about the Wise and Foolish Virgins teaches us that we should always be alert for the coming of the Lord. The story of the Pharisee and the Tax Collector praying in the temple warns us against self-righteousness. The parable of the Lost Sheep reminds us that the merciful God will seek us out even if we stray. We can appropriate these essential teachings without understanding all of the background or applying all of the details of the story.

Parables and Common Assumptions

We can also interpret the parables as poetic narratives, rich in metaphor, that convey fundamental assumptions about human existence. In the mid-1960s Amos Wilder, a poet as well as a theologian, challenged the well-established approach of Jülicher by insisting that the parables of Jesus are not pedagogical devices to teach a lesson. Rather, they are stories with odd twists that force us to rethink our common assumptions about life as a whole. They convey a vision of reality that cannot be reduced to logical analysis or conceptual categories. The parables function metaphorically, shocking our imaginations with the strangeness of the comparisons made. When Jesus originally told the story of the Good Samaritan, his Jewish audience would have been totally shocked that the hated foreigner was the one to assist their half-dead countryman. The shock prompts a reexamination of the whole question of who is the insider and who is the outsider and, more radically, whether such a distinction makes any sense at all. The philosopher Paul Ricoeur, who has had tremendous influence on biblical interpretation, explains the shocking character of the parables in terms of their metaphoric power to orient, disorient, and reorient us. In other words, they begin with a familiar pattern and then introduce a strange or surprising twist that disorients us and calls us to a new way of thinking and acting. Luke's story of the Wily Steward makes sense when the fired manager tries to ingratiate himself with his master's debtors by reducing their debts. But the disorienting shock occurs when the owner praises the fired manager for his behavior. Luke supplies us with one possible reorienting key when he suggests that we must be astute like the manager in pursuing the goals of the kingdom.

In order to appreciate the shocking character of the parables, we need to know more about Jewish life in first-century Palestine. Jesus talked about situations well known to his audience. It was dangerous to travel from Jerusalem to Jericho. Owners of vineyards had to hire extra day laborers at harvest time. Young Jewish men did take their inheritance and migrate to other countries. He used stock characters very familiar to his audience: prodigal sons, greedy landowners, insistent widows, and dishonest tax collectors. But Jesus usually injected material that was odd, strange, and unfamiliar. Owners of vineyards did not negotiate directly with workers, but did it through their stewards. Jewish fathers did not run out to greet their returning sons, whether wayward or not. Samaritans did not help wounded Jews. Shepherds did not leave the whole flock to search for one stray. Mustard seeds did not grow into large trees. A master going on a journey did not give his servants money equivalent to 150 years' wages. Sometimes a careful reading of a parable can reveal these oddities. We can figure out for ourselves that an owner of a vineyard would not send his son to negotiate with his tenants after they already abused and killed his servants. For other stories, we need a scholarly commentary to point out the strange twists: for example, *The Gospel in Parable* by John Donahue (Philadelphia: Fortress, 1988); *In Parables* by John Dominic Crossan (Sonoma, CA: Polebridge Press, 1992), and *Hear Then the Parable* by Bernard Brandon Scott (Minneapolis: Fortress, 1989). These authors help us discern the surprising elements in the parable that invite us to rethink our fundamental assumptions about life.

Reading Parables in Context

In preparing our homily we should take time to read the parables in context. Be attentive to what immediately precedes and follows them and how each of the evangelists uses them for his own distinct purpose. Mark highlights the difficulty of understanding the parables—even the disciples do not really grasp their deepest significance. This suggests that we must continue to probe the meaning of these enigmatic stories, allowing them to challenge our established perspectives and attitudes. Matthew's parables call us to discipleship and remind us that we stand under the judgment of God. This is most evident in his parable of the Last Judgment, in which individuals are saved or damned depending on whether they helped or ignored those in need. Reading Matthew today challenges our complacency and gives urgency to the task of following Christ. Luke often provides clues to his understanding of a particular parable. For instance, he introduces the story of the Pharisee and the Tax Collector with the note that it is for the benefit of those who "trusted in themselves that they were righteous and regarded others with contempt" (18:9). The realism of Luke's distinctive parables, such as the Good Samaritan and the Prodigal Son, invites us to participate in the story and to identify with the characters.

Parables and the Inner Life

A preacher can also use the parables to illumine and guide the internal struggle to become more mature Christians. In his book *The Kingdom Within* (Philadelphia: Lippincott, 1970), John Sanford, who has served as an Episcopal pastor and Jungian analyst, argues that the symbol of the kingdom points to the Spirit of God in our minds and hearts calling us to a greater integrity and authenticity. Interpreting the parable of the Prodigal Son from this perspective, he suggests that the two brothers symbolize two aspects of one whole personality. The elder brother represents a strong sense of duty and the desire to conform and please, while the younger represents a spontaneous and adventurous spirit. If the older brother dominates, a person becomes rigid and self-righteous. If the younger takes over, all discipline and restraint are lost. The father in the story represents the reconciling power of the kingdom. He attempts to reunite both sons by getting each one to face his one-sidedness and to incorporate the opposite characteristics. In the same way, the reign of God within us calls us to unite the more disciplined and the more spontaneous aspects of our own personalities in a fruitful and energizing synthesis. Following Sanford's lead, we could interpret all the parables as road maps for the inner journey. They call us to move toward greater integrity by bringing the unrecognized shadow side of our personalities into the light of consciousness.

Jesus was a master teacher. His parables are endlessly fascinating and supremely instructive. They deserve greater study and reflection. As preachers, we have the opportunity to probe their deeper meaning and to share the fruits of our reflection with the people we serve.

What Scripture Meant and Means Today

This examination of parables suggests that there is a distinction between what Scripture passages meant to the author and the original audience, and what they mean to us today and to our congregations. We can try to bridge this gap between what the passage meant and what it means in various ways. One extreme approach is to try to take the congregation back into the biblical world, so that the mind-set of the original author totally determines the message in the homily. The other extreme is to preach a contemporary message that has little connection with any of the meanings, literal or spiritual, contained in the text. Avoiding these extremes, most preachers set up some sort of dialogue, either explicitly or implicitly, between the text and themselves. This occurs naturally as we read the Scripture text and attempt to figure out what the passage has to say to people today. It is helpful to make this dialogic process more conscious by reflecting on its dynamics.

As we set up this conversation between ourselves and our congregation on the one side and the text on the other, we should begin with a deep respect for the Bible as the Word of God and the book of the church that contains a universal salvific message. Preachers who enter this conversation with open hearts expanded by regular prayer and meditation, and with critical minds tutored by study, have a better chance of mining the riches of the Scriptures. All classic texts have a surplus of meaning, but we grant a special, fuller sense to the Scriptures as an inexhaustible source of wisdom. The Bible, which is the normative witness to God's interaction with the human family, provides us with a framework for understanding human existence and motivation for transforming the world. In the conversation between Scripture and our current experience, the last word goes to the Bible. As preachers of the gospel, we pledge allegiance to Christ before expressing any other loyalties. The cross always remains judge of the flag.

A Mutually Critical Conversation

Following the lead of Catholic theologian David Tracy, we can think of our conversation with the scriptural passage as a mutually critical dialogue. In genuine dialogue, each partner can learn from the other and can criticize the other's position in the search for a greater understanding of the truth. In initiating a conversation with the Scriptures, we bring a whole set of assumptions drawn from our culture, our religious tradition, and our personal history. Our efforts to understand the text are influenced by our interests and the concerns of our congregation. Language is crucial to the act of interpretation. It reveals our worldview and points to the mystery at the heart of human existence. The way people speak about their significant joys and sorrows in life manifests their deeper attitudes and perspectives. As preachers, we need to listen well in order to understand the dreams and concerns of contemporary hearers of the Word. We also need to listen to our own characteristic ways of speaking for clues to the state of our souls. As the scriptures enter the conversation, they urge us to look more closely at our presuppositions. The biblical text may affirm our perceptions, challenge our assumptions, or move us to look more deeply at our hopes and concerns. In our listening, for example, we may hear a great deal of talk about feelings of insecurity resulting from the threat of terrorism, combined with a desire for revenge against those who attacked us. The story of the arrest of Jesus and his admonitions to put away the sword challenges the temptation to violence; it also suggests a more probing analysis of the roots of human insecurity and ways to deal with it from a faith perspective. To deepen the dialogue, preachers have to enter the biblical world, open themselves to the text, and try to participate in its meaning. We must bracket our own outlook and pass over to the standpoint of the author, trying to see the world through his eyes. Our hope is that we then return to our own standpoint enriched, both affirmed in some ways and challenged in others to broaden our horizons and to transform our lives. This is a difficult task, and we can easily distort or ignore the message of the text. We need to make a systematic effort to overcome these temptations, so that we can open our minds and hearts to the new possibility for a transformed life suggested by the text. This is one reason why remote preparation for preaching calls for personal development, which includes an effort to face honestly our blind spots and prejudices.

The Meaning in Front of the Text

When we enter into dialogue with a text, it then takes on a life of its own beyond the intention of the author. As the philosopher Paul Ricoeur puts it, the sense of the text is not just behind it but in front of it. The New Testament texts point to the historical Jesus, who proclaimed the kingdom, and to the future fulfillment of the reign of God. Thus, we can say that the world in front of biblical texts is really the kingdom of God, which is already here but is only gradually realized. This fuller meaning is disclosed as we address the Scripture passages with a new set of experiences and questions. Various interpretations will unavoidably emerge when we allow the passages to speak to our mind and heart. Not all will be equally valid, and some may violate the literal meaning of the text. We can test questionable interpretations by considering the overall meaning of the Bible as well as the way noted commentators understand the text. This approach preserves us, for instance, from interpreting the harsh statements of Jesus against the Pharisees as a justification for attacking Jews today or propagating subtle forms of anti-Semitism.

We should enter the dialogue with the Bible prepared for surprises and great challenges. Scripture passages may have a radical message for us—they may call for a totally different way of understanding human existence or of conducting ourselves as Christians. For instance, the parable of the workers who receive the same pay for one hour of work as those who bore the heat of the day could force a reconsideration of our whole success-oriented, competitive culture.

Troublesome Scripture Texts

The mutually critical conversation between the preacher and the Bible also includes criticisms of questionable passages from the perspective of contemporary developments. Once again, this inevitably happens when we encounter a controversial text such as the passage in Ephesians that enjoins women to be subordinate to their husbands (5:22). Without much thought, a homilist might decide to ignore it, or to point out that it comes from a patriarchal culture, or to reinterpret it in the light of the role of women in our society today. Making this process more explicit and consciously intentional enables us to make more careful judgments about bias within the scriptures and how to deal with it. It helps to remember that the books of the Bible are all written by men who lived in a patriarchal culture that accepted discrimination against various groups, including women, lepers, and slaves. As preachers, we have to be aware not only of obvious bias, such as Paul's admonition to Onesimus the slave to return to his master, but also of more subtle forms. The author of the book of Genesis, for example, seems to approve of Abraham's betrayal of his wife, Sarai, by pretending she was his sister, which saved himself but dragged Sarai into the king's harem.

The charge that the New Testament has an anti-Jewish bias deserves careful examination. We cannot ignore the horrible Christian history of persecution and mistreatment of Jews, often seemingly justified by gospel texts such as the response of the people to Pilate: "his blood be on us and on our children" (Matt 27:25). On the other hand, we must remember that the gospel material developed within a Jewish context and that attacks against "the Jews" were not anti-Semitic, but represented disputes within the Jewish world. The more we know about the sociological and cultural setting of the New Testament, as well as the intent of the author and the meaning of his words, the better equipped we are to handle the various forms of bias and ideology found in the texts.

As homilists, we enter the dialogue with biblical passages as members of the church that originally produced the Bible and that continues both to live under its normative judgment and to interpret it in the light of the developing life of the faith community. In dealing with difficult texts, we find guidance from various sources: for example, official documents that affirm a developing tradition, prophets who speak out against all forms of discrimination, Scripture scholars who place questionable passages in context, theologians who reinterpret and refocus traditional teaching, and ordinary believers who intuitively interpret individual passages in the light of the teaching of the Bible as a whole.

Thus, if we are wrestling with the troublesome verse enjoining women to be subordinate to their husbands, we recognize that many people in our congregation believe that God wants husbands and wives to relate on the basis of equality and mutual respect. Church leaders have issued official statements against sexism. Contemporary theologians insist that human beings are essentially interdependent and that personal growth is rooted in mutual giving and receiving. Scripture scholars remind us that Paul wrote in a patriarchal culture that assumed that the husband was the dominant partner in the marital relationship and could treat his wife in arbitrary ways. Paul moved beyond that model, however, by calling husbands to a self-sacrificing love of their wives modeled on the love of Christ for the church. Both husbands and wives should submit themselves to Christ, finding in the process not enslavement but a new sense of freedom. We could use these ideas to challenge a sexist interpretation of the text and turn it into a call for a new, liberating practice. All of this help and guidance enable us, when we prepare our homily, to have a more productive conversation with this text and other difficult passages.

Personal Engagement with the Scriptures

Interpreting Scripture is both a science and an art. Readily available commentaries on the Bible in general and the common lectionary in particular instruct us in the literal sense of the text and help us uncover the deeper meaning in the passages. The art of interpretation, however, still requires personal engagement with the Scriptures. We must read the biblical texts with prayerful hearts and paschal imaginations shaped by the death and resurrection of Jesus. In our conversation with a specific text, we hear, as well, voices from our congregation expressing their need for good news.

KEVIN ANDERSON RESPONSE

The importance of skillful interpretation of Scripture is clear. Our data indicate that listeners' responses to the item "This preacher helps me get a new or deeper appreciation of the Scripture readings" was ranked behind only "keeps my attention" and "knows what is in my heart" in ability to predict preacher effectiveness scores. The item "This preacher bases his/her preaching on the Scripture passages read at the service" was not as predictive, but was still positively correlated to preacher ratings.

Spiritual Hunger

There is much of value in Jim's comments to guide preachers in developing a professional sense about interpreting Scripture. People come to the service spiritually hungry. Like Frank, whom Jim mentioned in chapter 1 ("Father, I came here to Mass expecting to hear something in your sermon, and I listened carefully, but you never said anything"), people are actively looking for a little more light for the path. They want and need the preacher to be trained in Scripture scholarship and to be willing to put time in ahead of the homily to bring the Scriptures to light. A preacher who does last-minute preparation is more likely to show up with a dim flashlight than with a brightly burning lamp.

The Importance of Keeping Attention

Jim is right on target when he says that listeners hit the "shut-down" button pretty quickly when parables are treated with few new ideas or little imagination. This is the way the human brain works. It's as if there is a sentry in the brain that labels all incoming information as "new" or "familiar," and the familiar gets far less attention because it is simply routed directly to a preexisting category in the brain.

The importance of imagination in the homily addresses the number one predictor that we discovered in our studies of preaching effectiveness: holding the listener's attention. (The second strongest predictor, "knows what is in my heart," was discussed in the last chapter.) Nearly two-thirds of how listeners rate preachers can be accounted for by their response to the item "This preacher's style of delivering the sermon helps keep my attention." If we think of the homily as a telephone call from the preacher's mind to the listener's heart, attention is what puts the call through and the line that keeps it connected. Once the listener's attention is lost, there's nothing but a dial tone, and whatever the preacher is saying is no longer getting through.

Jesus was a master at holding attention because he knew the power of stories. He also seemed to know intuitively that an enigmatic story has greater staying power than one that can be easily and completely explained and then forgotten. We are drawn back to the parables because they have a power that is born of their often puzzling nature. Jim's discussion of how the parables "shock our imaginations with the strangeness of the connections made" provides an opportunity to elaborate on an important determiner of whether a listener will attend to the preacher and whether the preacher's message will be remembered beyond a few hours after it was delivered. I'm talking about the "deep processing" theory of attention and memory.

The Deep Processing Theory

Psychologists have known for decades that stimuli that force the brain to process new or strange images or ideas are attended to and remembered unusually well. The greater the number of experiential modalities in which a message is communicated, the higher is the chance that it will be attended to and remembered. For instance, parables are stories that create images, contain unexpected twists, and leave us often with a sense of unfinishedness. This causes the brain to spend time processing them far longer than a simple, logical input. The result of the longer, deeper processing is much greater duration for the "memory trace" that is created in the brain.

The deep processing theory of memory may help explain why humor is a top ten predictor of preaching effectiveness. Nearly half of variability in preacher ratings can be accounted for by knowing a listener's response to the item "This preacher uses humor effectively in sermons." Humor that works combines a relevant human story with a surprise ending that wakes the mind up, holds attention, and produces delight. Homilists who pepper their sermons with humor without allowing the humor to obscure the Scripture readings or the human concern being addressed are likely to keep listeners on their toes. Humor is a basic human form of interaction that is capable of getting and keeping a listener's attention.

Preachers can model their own approach to spiritual teaching after that of Jesus, remembering to shock the often-slumbering human imagination to attention. The stranger the image or idea, the better it will be remembered. This does not mean that preachers should go for pure shock value without meaningful content. It just means that we need to get away from the boring, the predictable, the tried and true, the safe ways of preaching. Staying within already formed categories in the brain gives the homilist two strikes against him or her, regardless of how much time has gone into preparation.

My children remind me occasionally about the best homily they ever saw. Fr. Mark, a priest at a local parish, performed a magic act during the homily and spoke eloquently about its message for knowing God. The children's attention was riveted, and their processing of his message was deep. Humor, stories, poetry, quotations, singing, magic, whatever else can shock the imagination—these are not just nice extras to consider including occasionally in a homily. They are usually the difference between a message that is only moderately attended to and quickly forgotten and one that commands attention and lives in a listener's mind long after the homily is over.

Thinking Allegorically

Reading Jim's discussion of allegorical interpretation of Scripture, I was reminded of what I tell clients about dreams. There are multiple ways to interpret a dream. We cannot prove that any interpretation is the right one. An attitude of using dream material to spur creative reflection on one's life is the whole point of working with dreams. It seems that a similar approach to Scripture could produce new and memorable ways for listeners to relate to Scripture. We don't have to claim that the author of the text intended it to be allegorical. The exercise of thinking allegorically is itself a deep processing activity that helps listeners integrate their spiritual knowledge or experience.

Composite Characters

Jim points out that Jesus used stock characters familiar to the people to whom he spoke. In his homilies, Jim often uses modern-day stock or composite characters—a person (real or aggregated from experiences of several people) to whose stories they can say, "Yes, I know that experience." Just as Jesus made sure that his listeners could relate to the stories he told, modern preachers are challenged to do the same. Composite characters allow the experience of the congregation to be reflected back to them in the homily while at the same time preserving confidentiality.

Relevance

If, speaking for modern-day listeners, I could say one thing to preachers regarding their treatment of Scripture, it would be this: Don't just shed light on the Scripture passages; be creative about helping us see how the Scripture passages shed light on the joys and difficulties of our attempts to walk a spiritual path through life. This is Jim's major emphasis in the next chapter: that the focus of the homily emerges from a "dialogue" between the Scripture readings and the human concerns of the people in the pews. Our data indicate that relating the homily to daily life is crucial. A listener's response to the item "This preacher's sermons are relevant to my daily life" is a top five predictor of preacher ratings, capable of accounting by itself for over half of the variability in preacher effectiveness scores.

JAMES BACIK RESPONSE

Kevin provides a practical slant on the task of interpreting Scripture by emphasizing the importance of holding the attention of the congregation. He encourages us to find fresh ways of presenting the familiar biblical material so that it not only engages the congregation but remains longer in their active memory. Kevin has a great sense of the power of the new and the different in biblical preaching, especially when the homily is part of a traditional liturgical celebration. While serving as ministry assistant at Corpus Christi University Parish, he devised a Holy Thursday liturgy featuring small-group dialogue homilies. Parishioners sit around tables and discuss the meaning for them of the gospel passage that portrays Jesus washing the feet of the disciples at the Last Supper (John 13:1–15). I set the stage for the dialogue with some questions: for instance, were there times during this past year when you, like Peter, were reluctant to have your feet washed? I also listen to the discussion at one table and report that back to the whole assembly. For two decades now, we have continued to use this format for eliciting fresh thinking on the familiar story of the washing of the feet. This Holy Thursday celebration remains one of our most engaging liturgies of the year, in part because it provides a different context for reflecting personally on the scriptural message.

Kevin's call for innovative approaches to interpreting Scripture stands in dialectical tension with the normative function of the Bible. For Christians, the Bible is the privileged witness to God's saving activity in the world and has guided the life of the faith community through the centuries. The familiar words of Scripture have comforted and challenged the faithful in diverse cultures and historical periods. The literal meaning of the text grounds and guides the efforts to discern a fuller sense. The classic interpretations of particular passages have borne the test of time. Within the liturgical setting, the familiar and the expected set the stage for personal reflection. This is not to deny the value of new and striking approaches to preaching the Word. Surely, Kevin makes an important point about creative ways of gaining and keeping the attention of the congregation. We do this best when we keep in mind the normative character of the Bible.

CHAPTER FIVE

Determining the Focus and Function of Your Homily

Now that we have considered issues of remote preparation for preaching, let us turn to the more proximate task of determining the focus for a particular homily and its function. This discussion expands and applies the general principles of interpretation established in the previous chapter.

A Thematic Approach

Books on preaching commonly advise a process of preparation centered on coming up with a theme for the homily. For example: spend time praying over the Scripture readings and studying them, determine a broad theme found in the readings, gather ideas around the theme, narrow the theme and come up with a central idea that can be expressed in a single sentence that captures the main point. Many preachers follow some version of this thematic approach. It might be as simple as finding a good idea in the Scripture passages and developing it. Others employ a more elaborate method: for example, reading commentaries on the passage that suggest a number of possible themes, choosing the one that seems most appropriate, tracing the development of the theme in the Bible, and determining how this central idea applies today. This thematic approach comes rather naturally for preachers who are using the common lectionary, since the first and third readings, along with the responsorial psalm, and sometimes the second reading, are linked thematically. Those who do not follow the lectionary generally choose the Scripture readings with a central idea or common theme in mind. We can imagine a beautifully constructed homily on the theme of covenant that recalls successively God's covenant with the Israelites in the experience of the exodus, the prophecy of Jeremiah about a new covenant written on the heart, the fulfillment of that prophecy in Jesus, who established the new covenant of love, and, finally, the way in which the new law of love is manifest in the covenant of marriage.

While the thematic approach, whether simple or elaborate, has some advantages, especially fidelity to the Scriptures, it runs the danger of appearing irrelevant to the lives of the hearers of the Word. The central idea in the readings may not have much intrinsic meaning for people today. The theme linking the Scripture passages may be foreign to the contemporary mind-set. A man hearing the beautifully constructed homily on marriage as a covenant may be wondering what this has to do with his daily struggle to hold his marriage together. No doubt, some thematic preachers sense the problem and do an admirable job of overcoming the danger of sounding irrelevant. Even this determined effort, however, highlights the flawed character of the thematic methodology, which is not well designed to make connections between the Scripture readings and the contemporary situation.

Determining a Focus Point

An alternative to the thematic approach is to determine a focus point for the homily. The focus point arises out of a conversation between particular Scripture passages and the current experiences of the congregation, shared and articulated by the homilist. This approach develops, in a specific way, the mutually critical dialogue between Scripture and contemporary life that we advocated in chapter 4. It is rooted in the theological conviction that God speaks to us not only through the Scriptures but in and through our whole life in the world. A focus point must include both insights from the Scripture readings and an existential concern or significant issue, such as the quest for knowledge and love, the joys and disappointments of personal relationships, and the opportunities and challenges of life in society. Determining a focus point is not as simple as getting a good idea from the

Scripture passages and developing it. It flows from a conversation that requires prayerful reflection and careful attention to God's Word as heard in a particular biblical text, in the lives of the people we serve, and in our own hearts. Not only does this method, which draws the homilist into the process, have the inherent advantage of beginning with the explicit relevance of the Scripture texts to the congregation; it also calls for an effort to describe the existential concern in terms familiar to our people, a point we will develop in chapter 6.

Here is an attempt to articulate a focus point for the Second Sunday of Easter in Cycle B, which features the passage from John's Gospel about doubting Thomas (John 20:19–31). In the midst of all the ways in which we experience alienation and separation—as Thomas experienced because he was absent when Jesus appeared the first time—Jesus says to us: "Peace be with you" (as he did to Thomas), which invites us into a deeper experience of community. This focus calls for a good description of the ways we experience separation: for example, being the black sheep in the family, being single in a society that caters to couples, being divorced in a church that celebrates successful marriages. It also demands an exploration of the inclusive, integrating power of the peace offered by Christ to Thomas and to us. This focus point implicitly reflects the experience of the homilist in dealing with estrangement and separation: for instance, the gulf created by unrealistic expectations of our congregation as well as the concrete instances when Christ's reconciling grace overcame that gap. This focus is obviously more complex than developing the theme of faith based on the example of Thomas, but it has the advantage of drawing the congregation into reflection on the common human experience of estrangement.

Interpreting the Scripture Readings in Context

The internal dialogue that produces a focus point has its own inner logic and integrity. It is helpful, however, to distinguish for analysis three components: Scripture, common experience, and the dialogue between them.

First, we have the task of interpreting the Scripture readings that form the basis for a specific homily. As we saw in the previous chapter, we must interpret these passages in the light of the Bible as a whole and in the light of other Scripture texts. If our initial reading of the text suggests a focus that is opposed to the general thrust of biblical teaching, then we have a solid basis for rejecting that insight and searching for an alternative. A preacher tempted to use John's characterization of "the Jews" as the opponents of Jesus in order to promote the "Jews for Jesus" movement ought to consider Paul's outlook on the enduring role of the Jews as God's people (Rom 11:25–29). Although the story of Jesus forgiving the woman taken in adultery (John 8:1–11) might initially suggest a homily restricted to the question of personal forgiveness, we could broaden the focus by recalling the ways Jesus the liberator challenged the patriarchy and sexism of his own time.

Examining the Scripture texts in the context of the liturgical seasons is also helpful. This is obviously important for lectionary-based preaching, but it also applies to selecting texts for particular seasons. Determining focus points for a whole season at a single planning session not only avoids repetition, but also allows for a more comprehensive treatment of themes common to the season.

Scripture passages read in the context of communal worship often take on a fuller meaning that suggests a distinctive focal point. Passages from the sixth chapter of John read at Eucharistic celebrations might well suggest a homily on the way Christ, the Bread of Life, satisfies the common human hungers for community as well as for spiritual nourishment.

When we are determining a focus, we should take into account all the assigned Scripture passages. The lectionary generally links the first reading, the psalm, and the third reading thematically and sometimes includes the second reading as well. Determining a focal point is more difficult than picking up on the theme already suggested in the choice of readings. Sometimes the other readings suggest a slant on a focus suggested by the Gospel. On the first Sunday of Lent in Cycle B, Mark's very succinct account of the temptation (1:12–15) suggests a struggle with demonic forces, but leaves open the nature and specifics of the conflict. The first reading (Gen 9:8–15), which describes God's covenant after the flood, suggests the cosmic nature of the conflict with the dark forces, while the second reading (1 Pet 3:18–22) points to the internal struggle to maintain a clear conscience. Thus, we might focus on the way Christ guides and strengthens us by his example and teaching to handle the unavoidable struggles against large cosmic and social evils as well as our personal demons.

At times the first reading will determine the choice of one focus over other possibilities in the Gospel. The Gospel for the Fourth Sunday of Lent (John 9:1–41), which recounts the cure of the man blind from birth, is rich with possible focus points, including the temptation to religious hypocrisy as represented by the Pharisees. The second reading for the day, from Ephesians 5:18–24, which calls us to live as children of the light, suggests a homily on the power of Christ to cure the kind of spiritual blindness that fails to see the light of grace in the darkness of everyday life.

Intention of the Texts

In trying to comprehend the meaning of individual Scripture passages, it helps to ask what human concern the author was addressing or, more modestly, what concern the text as we know it addresses. Since there are obvious problems in determining the actual intention of the biblical authors, it is better to consider the issues behind the text. What human concern, what existential issue, what social problem does the text address either directly or indirectly?

In searching the gospel passage for a focus, we should keep in mind the distinction between what Jesus originally said and did (as well as it can be reconstructed by scholars) and what was intended by the evangelist. The parable of the Sower and the Seed (Matt 13:1–23), which appears in the lectionary on the Fifteenth Sunday of Ordinary Time Cycle A, offers two possible focus points based on this distinction. Scholars tell us that the parable as originally told by Jesus emphasized the all-inclusive love of God, who scatters the seed generously, offering the Word to all people. From this perspective we could focus on the teaching of Jesus that challenges our temptation to exclude others from God's circle of love. The explanation of the parable (13:18–23), added by the evangelist, calls the hearers to overcome various impediments and become fertile soil for the Word. A focus based on this part of the text might explore the diverse ways in which we impede God's Word, as well as the ways Christ helps us become more receptive hearers of the Word. By trying to discern the intent implied in the text, we have a better chance of finding an insight that will prove relevant to people today.

Concerns of the Congregation

The process of developing a focus point must also consider the other partner to the conversation, the members of the congregation and their significant concerns. As we saw in chapter 3, the homilist needs to be aware of what the hearers of the Word are feeling and thinking, what grabs their attention and sparks their interest, what causes them to reflect and moves them to action, what keeps them awake at night and gets them up in the morning, what brings them satisfaction and what makes them feel guilty, what challenges and energizes them. We need to understand people's dreams, hopes, and goals as well as their nightmares, frustrations, and failures so that their concerns are represented in the dialogue with the biblical passages.

Congregational concerns flow out of both positive and negative experiences. A man blessed with material wealth may be concerned about how to offer fitting thanks and how to share his blessings with others. A young widow may be concerned about how she's going to live as a single person in her couple-oriented social world. Because pastoral leaders tend to hear more about the negative experiences of their people, they must stay alert for concerns that flow from more positive experiences. Some people express their concerns in the form of questions: Why am I depressed? How can I help my friend who is ill? What can I do to improve my prayer life? Others make declarative statements that imply a concern: My wife is such a great example to me. I am not getting much out of Sunday worship. One guy I work with really gets on my nerves. Each case poses the question of how to respond to the given situation.

The Preacher's Experience

In determining the concerns of the congregation, we, as preachers, do well to include our own experiences. We are, after all, members of the church and hearers of the Word, standing under the judgment of the gospel. We must know our own hearts in order to know the hearts of others, as suggested by the motto of John Henry Newman: *Cor ad cor loquitur*, "Heart speaks to heart." Our own efforts to follow Christ in the various dimensions of our lives are likely to reflect the experiences of our people. If we feel better and function more efficiently when we exercise regularly, we can assume that others do also. Our efforts to rise above anger and frustration no doubt resonate with the people we serve. A preacher who is battling low self-esteem can speak authentically about a cross borne by many others. If we have worked hard to acquire a particular virtue, then we know something of the common struggle to live more virtuously. Our joy in learning more about the faith leads us to think that some individuals and groups will also find the experience satisfying. The homilist's unique relationship with Christ makes it possible to recognize the various ways other hearers of the Word relate to the Lord.

Cultural and Historical Influences

Preachers attentive to the cultural influences on the congregation described in chapter 3 will more readily discern their real concerns. Christians today have to figure out how to maintain a sense of the common good in an individualistic culture; how to avoid greed in a consumer society; how to stay focused in the midst of multiple demands on time and energy; how to function as good citizens in a country tempted by the arrogance of power. Historical developments also create distinctive concerns: How should we respond to fellow believers who want everyone to return to the rigid approaches of the past? What is the proper role of science in creating a more humane world? How do we maintain standards of truth and goodness in a postmodern world filled with relativism? What can be done to maintain healthy communities in an electronic age dominated by impersonal technology?

Communal Life

Many human concerns flow from communal life. By its very nature, family life creates deep joys and great challenges. Parents want a good education for their children. Grandparents delight in their grandchildren. Spouses can wound their partners as well as love them. Teenagers influenced by the youth culture desire greater freedom. The family circle generates a great many common concerns charged with strong emotion and expressed with endless variation.

Our work, usually done in communal settings, generates a special set of concerns suggested by common comments of workers: My work is boring. I love my job. One of my colleagues makes me feel inferior. My fellow workers were so supportive when I was sick. With all the demands at work, I have little time for my family. I am underpaid for all the work I do. In these tough economic times, my job is not very secure. My company encourages charitable giving by matching my contributions. My work as a volunteer is very satisfying. Sometimes I wonder if anyone appreciates the skill and effort needed to raise children. My work brings me closer to God. I see very little connection between my faith and my work. Parishioners who put so much time and energy into their work need to hear homilies that address this area of their lives.

Hearers of the preached Word have concerns arising from their participation in a faith community. How can I get more out of the worship service? How can I use my gifts and talents to build up the church? What am I to make of the sins and failures of the church? How can I gain a more mature understanding of the faith? What percentage of my income should I contribute to the church? What role should the congregation play in promoting justice and helping the needy? How can the local church promote the spiritual growth of its members? Do the homilies challenge me to apply gospel ideals to everyday life? How can we avoid factions in the church and promote a search for common ground? How can I best give thanks for the ways the parish supports and challenges me? Although homilists have to maintain a broad vision of human concerns, we still cannot avoid periodically addressing congregational issues.

As citizens of the country, Christians have to relate to cultural trends and social institutions. Does my faith ever challenge the assumptions of the dominant culture? Do I participate in the political process? What form does the virtue of patriotism take for citizens of the world's lone superpower? What principles of Christian social teaching guide my positions on questions of public policy? Do I belong to any voluntary associations (for example, Bread for the World) that work for the common good? What should I be doing to promote reconciliation, harmony, and peace in my neighborhood, my city, my country, and the world? As homilists, we have the task of ensuring that the large issues are not totally submerged by the daily demands of ordinary life.

The Tensions of Life

Preachers can also discover important concerns by reflecting on the common tensions people experience today. Individuals know the struggle to balance or integrate competing interests and demands: between reason and emotion; between faith commitments and openness to other traditions; between hopeful dreams and harsh realities. Spouses must balance their calling to care for their partner with their own need to receive affirmation and love. At times, friends are forced to choose between self-interest and the needs of the other. Parents must combine compassionate love with firm discipline in raising their children. Young people know the tension between peer pressure and traditional moral norms. Many people struggle to balance time commitments among job, family, and personal needs. Serious Christians know the daily struggle to live the gospel in a culture shaped not only by high ideals but also by consumerism, individualism, and materialism.

Sex and Money

A homilist has to pay special attention to questions surrounding sexuality and money—two areas that generate strong feelings and are too seldom addressed from a Christian perspective. How do believers achieve and maintain a healthy outlook on sex in a church tinged with puritanism and a culture that considers sex to be an autonomous possession and restraint abnormal?

What attitude should Christians who live in an affluent country have toward money, and how can we use our wealth to serve the needs of others and the common good? These fundamental questions raise a great variety of more specific concerns that are on our people's minds and need to be addressed from the viewpoint of the gospel.

Keeping in mind common experience, community life, and the tensions of daily existence, we preachers can discern the real concerns of our people so their interests are properly represented in the conversation with the Scripture readings.

The Dialogue between Scripture and the Contemporary Situation

In determining the focus for a particular homily, the next step is to relate the scriptural texts to the situation of the congregation. As indicated in chapter 4, we can think of this as a mutually critical dialogue between the text and the hearers of the Word. This conversation takes place in our mind and heart as, in the process of preparing our homily, we relate our critical understanding of the Scriptures to the interests and concerns of the people we serve. Preachers intent on communicating the scriptural Word to their congregations enter this process automatically. While it is as simple as pondering how this gospel encourages and challenges people today, we can enrich this process by exploring the dynamics of the conversation, guided by insights from theological hermeneutics, the discipline that treats the interpretation of sacred texts.

Hermeneutical Theory

Modern hermeneutics began with the work of the great Protestant theologian Friedrich Schleiermacher (1768–1834), who raised philosophical questions about interpreting texts and insisted on a personal appropriation of the Scriptures that is always mediated through language and never exhausts the meaning of the text. Theologians have benefited from dialogue with philosophical hermeneutics, especially the work of Martin Heidegger (1889–1976), who notes that we always enter the "hermeneutical circle" influenced by our own interests and assumptions; Hans-Georg Gadamer (1900–2002), who insists that interpreters respect the text and enter into the tradition it represents through a "fusion of horizons"; Paul Ricoeur (1913–), who points out that texts have a life of their own and contain a fuller meaning beyond the intent of the author; and Jacques Derrida (1930–2004), proponent of the deconstructionist view that the meanings of texts are fluid and authoritative interpretations are oppressive.

Practical Advice

From these authors and other leaders in the field, we can glean ten practical suggestions for a more effective conversation in search of a focus point:

1. Since the scriptural texts are for us the Word of God, we should approach them with respect and prepare for the conversation through prayerful reflection.

2. The texts cannot defend themselves in this dialogue, so homilists should be careful not to impose their own bias and limited perspectives on them. Rather, as Gadamer suggests, we should submit ourselves to the passages like an athlete submits herself to the rules of the game. In this process, we should be open to surprising meanings that emerge in the conversation.

3. A mutually critical conversation demands that preachers avoid focus points that uncritically reflect questionable cultural assumptions found in the Bible, such as a patriarchal bias.

4. For effective dialogue, homilists can and must pass over to the biblical world. This point requires further explanation. The biblical passages reflect a distinctive world that is in many ways unfamiliar to us. Between us and the text there is a historical and cultural distance, so that the intention of the biblical authors is generally not immediately available

to us. Nevertheless, we should try to pass over to their world and become familiar with its important figures, its dominant symbols, its cultural assumptions, and its societal ideals. To do this, we must suspend our usual categories and perspectives and see the world through the lens of the Scripture passages. Although we can never pass over completely to that other world and we always return to our own standpoint, the effort can be fruitful. It enriches our own viewpoint and often reveals common concerns. We can fuse horizons (bring two worldviews into fruitful dialogue) because the biblical world has helped shape our own and because our most personal concerns have a universal character. For example, people in the biblical world had to deal with the fragile and precarious nature of human existence, with illness, suffering, and death, as do we. The preacher who tries to pass over to the world reflected in the text has a better chance of finding a fresh and effective focus.

5. In preparing our homily, we should pay careful attention to the language and structure of the Scripture readings. As Schleiermacher and Ricoeur insist, language is the key to interpretation. To take a familiar example, Romans 8:14–17 contrasts a spirit of slavery and fear with a spirit of adoption that allows us to cry "*Abba,* Father." Realizing that the Aramaic *Abba* suggests endearment, a homilist could emphasize the remarkably intimate relationship with God that enables us to overcome various types of enslaving fear. The preacher who knows Paul's distinction between *sarx* (the Greek word translated as "flesh" that refers to all the forces that carry us away from God) and *pneuma* (translated as "spirit," referring to the total self under the sway of the Holy Spirit) will not restrict a homily on Romans 8:1–13 to an attack on sexual immorality. For preachers who lack a sufficient knowledge of Hebrew and Greek, the standard commentaries often highlight the original meaning of key words as well as the flow of thoughts within the passage, and this can trigger reflection on possible focus points.

6. In our conversation, we should look for the pattern of concern and response already contained in the biblical passages. The Scriptures present high ideals and call for a great variety of transformations, new ways of envisioning our relationship to God, fresh perspectives on the ultimate meaning of life, healthier attitudes, a deeper spirituality, and more effective efforts to spread the reign of God in the world. Focus points must include responses to concerns: ways of dealing with problems, suggested courses of action, constructive perspectives, supports for doing good, challenges to conversion, and hopes for the future. Occasionally the connection between concern and response is explicit. In Luke's Gospel, for instance, Jesus tells the parable of the Good Samaritan in response to the question, Who is my neighbor (10:25–37)? More commonly, we have to discover the concern implicit in the text and make the connection ourselves so that the marvelous wisdom and inspiring idealism of the Bible can emerge as relevant for people today.

7. In dialoguing with the Scriptures, we preachers should consider not only our own concerns but those of the faith community as well. We enter Heidegger's hermeneutical circle with our personal interests and pastoral responsibilities. Regular self-examination gradually reveals the specific contours of our own virtues and vices, our insights and oversights, our strengths and weakness, our areas of interest, and those that regularly escape our radar screen. Enlightened by self-criticism, we can be attentive to possible focus points that not only confirm our own perspectives and strengths, but also challenge us to conversion in needed areas. Our understanding and appreciation of the concerns of the people we serve enrich the conversation and broaden the search for a focus. When this works well, celibate homilists pay attention to family concerns, male preachers consider women's issues, senior pastors take seriously the interests of young people, and those with a private piety take into account the passion of social activists. Some homilists

find they do a better job of discerning helpful focal points when they participate in a group discussion of the readings for the following Sunday and observe which points grab the attention of the participants.

8. The process of discerning a focus demands openness and flexibility. Paul Ricoeur reminds us that our conversation with the biblical text may alter or deepen our original concern and initial focus. In considering the story of the Prodigal Son, for example, we may begin by thinking that our homily should highlight the amazing availability of forgiving grace for those who have willfully squandered their resources. Further reflection, however, may move us to focus on the problem of rigidity (represented by the elder son) and the invitation to forgiving acceptance of others. The homilist who stays open to this process often finds a fresh and challenging focus.

9. Realizing the richness of the biblical texts, a preacher can avoid the trap of spending excessive time searching for the perfect focus point. Although deconstructionist theory leads to an unacceptable total relativism, Jacques Derrida and others offer a useful reminder that the readings yield more than one focus point and that no one focus exhausts these possibilities. In the conversation between text and situation, we are free to look for a relatively adequate focus that is faithful to the Scriptures and responsive to the people's needs. This is good news for homilists who follow the lectionary, because it means we can preach to the same congregation on the same readings every third year and keep coming up with a new focus.

10. For the sake of clarity, we should write down the focus point. The common hermeneutic distinction between understanding a text and explaining it encourages a clear and precise articulation of the insights that flow from our own reflection. The conversation between the meaning of specific scriptural passages and the concrete needs of the congregation, which takes initial form in our own mind and heart, often achieves greater clarity as we attempt to articulate our understanding to others. The

attempt to write down the focus may reveal its limitations and force us to refine it or perhaps to start the process over. If we cannot come up with a brief, coherent explanation of the focus, it probably will not work as the basis for a homily.

Two Examples

We can make this advice for determining a focus more concrete with an example.

A pastor was going to preach to his congregation on a single passage, the calming of the storm in Mark 4:35–41. A week ahead of time, he began his search for a focus immediately after his daily centering prayer, which helped clear his mind and lift his heart. In a reflective mood, he slowly read the passage and then decided to do a few more minutes of Ignatian-style meditation, imaginatively placing himself in the boat with Jesus, who is asleep, and the disciples, including the veteran fishermen, who are terrified.

The pastor's imagination quickly produced a vivid scene from his youth when he was fishing with his father and the lake became very rough, and, for the first time in his life, he saw fear in the face of his father, who was a very poor swimmer. This helped him appreciate in a new way the dynamics of the interaction between the disciples and Jesus. The verse that struck him, however, was the question of the disciples: Who, then, is this whom even wind and sea obey? The pastor recognized a typical Markan theme, the remarkable inability of the disciples to identify Jesus properly despite numerous clues. In Mark, Jesus is indeed a hidden Messiah. Sensing a possible focus, the pastor began reflecting on ways he himself has trouble recognizing Jesus in his daily ministry, especially when burdened by stressful situations. He also recalled ways in which members of his congregation fail to identify Christ in their lives, especially by excluding his challenging message from the business world and the political arena.

With this in mind, the pastor read the short section in the *New Jerome Biblical Commentary* that suggests that this miracle story reveals the power of Jesus over Satan operative in nature. In the ancient Near East, the raging sea represented the power of chaos and evil that struggles against God. In calming the sea, Jesus manifests divine power and then rebukes the disciples for their lack of faith, which could be interpreted as referring either to God or to himself. The pastor liked the idea that it referred to Jesus himself because it fit in better with his emerging focus point. Satisfied that his insight was faithful to the meaning of the text, he made an initial effort to formulate the focus: If we recognize the true nature of Christ, we would be less likely to exclude him and his powerful message from important areas of our lives.

Not totally satisfied with this formulation, the pastor knew he would have to return to it and looked forward to getting some help at the weekly staff meeting, when he and his colleagues would have their regular discussion of the readings for the following Sunday. In the discussion, the first comment came from a woman who summarized Monika Hellwig's comment in *Gladness Their Escort* (Wilmington, DE: Michael Glazier, 1987) that the waters of chaos threaten our world today in the form of war, famine, corruption, cruelty, injustice, and oppression. The other staff members immediately gravitated to the symbol of the storm representing the forces that threaten to overwhelm us today. No one brought up the concern over the identity of Jesus, and everyone had something to say about the storms of life.

At that point, the pastor knew he would have to rethink the focus for the homily. He made a mental note to consult the *Anchor Bible* commentary on Mark, especially to check the Greek words translated as "terrified" and "awe," but he never got around to doing it. He did go back to the passage with the storm image in mind as well as the panicked look on his father's face. He recalled a retreat when the majority of the participants chose the calming of the storm as their favorite miracle story because it provided comfort in the midst of the storms threatening to submerge them. At the retreat, a mother described the chaos in her life created by two teenage boys bent on achieving instant autonomy. A teacher spoke of being overwhelmed by inattentive students and demanding parents. As more recent examples of parishioners threatened by the various storms of life came to his mind, the pastor decided to shift the focus away from the identity of Jesus to the power of Christ. His revised focus point read: In the midst of the storms of life that threaten to submerge us, we can count on the power of Christ to give us the strength and guidance needed to cope with them.

This example demonstrates many of the important moves in coming up with a focus point: set up a conversation between text and situation and enter it prayerfully; be faithful to the meaning of the Scriptures; see the Scripture passage in the light of the whole book; be attentive to the words, symbols, and structure of the reading; take seriously the needs of the congregation; look for the pattern of concern and response in the passage; share in a group discussion of the reading; allow the conversation to influence the choice of focus; write down the focus point.

We can imagine a much simpler version of the same process:

> A very busy pastor, committed to preaching sermons that are not "back there" or "up there" but pertain to the real life issues of her congregation, sets aside an hour for homily preparation, choosing for her text the calming of the storm in Mark. After saying the Lord's Prayer, she reads the passage over a couple of times slowly and thoughtfully. In the process, she recalls a man saying that if it wasn't for prayer he would have long ago drowned under the pressure of his job. At that point, the focus of the homily begins to form in her mind. She checks her intuition by consulting her favorite commentary, *Preaching the Lectionary* by Reginald Fuller, who suggests proclaiming the power of Christ to still storms today for those who cling to him.
>
> This clinches the direction of the sermon. She will talk about the importance of faith in Christ to avoid being submerged by the rough waves of life. The important point is that this pastor did not come up with a theme, such as prayer or the power of Jesus. Rather, she found a focus point that included an existential concern and an important biblical insight. Even busy pastors who have no time to study modern hermeneutics can preach more effectively by consciously and explicitly relating the biblical texts to the interests and concerns of their people.

Focus Points for a Liturgical Season

In developing focus points, we can avoid overlap and achieve a more comprehensive treatment of common concerns and biblical teachings by keeping a list of our previous homilies and planning ahead for whole liturgical seasons. Let us imagine a pastor who follows the common lectionary choosing focus points for Year A of the Advent season:

While reflecting on the readings for the first Sunday (Isa 2:1–5; Rom 13:11–14; Matt 24:34–44), the pastor intends initially to focus on the call to walk in the light of the Lord in order to cast off the deeds of darkness that blind us to God's glory and the possibilities for personal growth. Checking his records, he finds that he preached on this very point three years ago. He cannot imagine that anyone in the congregation really remembers, but for the sake of balance and variety, he looks for another possibility, finally settling on the mandate to work for peace (beat swords into plowshares) that challenges our complacency and cynicism.

Looking ahead, the pastor notes that John the Baptist appears in the Gospels for both the second and third Sundays and decides to focus on him on the second Sunday. On the basis of the readings (Isa 11:1–10; Rom 15:4–9; Matt 3:1–12), he emphasizes John's pointed message to each one of us to give evidence of reform, even though harsh demands may make us feel guilty or induce rationalization (common concerns). On the third Sunday (Isa 35:1–6a,10; Jas 5:7–10; Matt 11:2–11), he concentrates on the often neglected book of James, highlighting the need for patience in dealing with the frustrations of life. The fourth Sunday (Isa 7:11–14; Rom 1:1–7; Matt 1:18–24) offers the opportunity to reflect on the contrast between Joseph, who is open to the call of God in an extremely complex and confusing situation, and Ahaz, who represents the common temptation to respond to God on the basis of our own limited understanding.

Let us consider another example of planning ahead. During the eight Sundays from Easter to Pentecost that constitute the Easter season, we reflect on the meaning of the resurrection from various perspectives. In Cycle B the readings from John stress our intimate relationship with Christ, as we consider him interacting with Thomas and presenting himself as the good shepherd, the true vine, the exemplar of love, and the sender of the Advocate. On Good Shepherd Sunday, we might avoid the obvious intimacy suggested by the image and instead address the state of the ecumenical movement in the light of Christ's call for one flock and one shepherd. This allows us to concentrate on our intimate relationship to Christ on the following Sunday, when the image of the vine and the branches suggests that we can live more effectively in a challenging environment by drawing on the strength and energy of Christ, the true vine. Keeping records and planning ahead takes time and energy, but it pays off in a more diverse and comprehensive selection of focus points.

The Function of a Homily

Turning to the second major point of this chapter: homilies should have an explicit function as well as a clear focus. An effective homily not only conveys meaning but also accomplishes something. As the linguistic analysts insist, language is performative. It not only signifies; it also performs some function. Biblical texts speak to us of God's saving activity and also call for a change of heart. Homilies should reflect this scriptural pattern. Effective preachers clarify for themselves what they are trying to accomplish in a given homily. They decide on a function as well as a focus.

In general, homilies promote some kind of transformation— broader horizons, deeper commitments, better behavior. We can specify this by recalling Lonergan's categories of conversion in various dimensions of human existence: physical, emotional, imaginative, intellectual, moral, and religious. Thus we could envision a Lenten homily designed to transform poor eating habits through regular fasting; a Pentecost homily showing how the Spirit can transform hard hearts into compassionate ones; a homily based on 1 John to transform harsh images of God into more loving ones; an Advent homily aimed at transforming an exclusive notion of salvation into a more inclusive understanding of God's will to save all people; a sermon on the great commandment to transform selfish behavior into a generous love of neighbor; an Easter homily intended to transform dull religious sensibilities into a lively sense of Christ's abiding presence.

In one sense, all Christian preaching has the function of bringing people closer to Jesus Christ. This more intimate relationship could be specified in various ways: to put on the mind of Christ; to become more committed disciples of the Lord; to appropriate the wisdom of the great Teacher; to imitate the Man for others; to accept Jesus as our Savior; to believe in Jesus as the Son of God; to worship the cosmic Christ; to hear the voice of the Good Shepherd;

to heed the commands of the definitive Prophet; to tap the energy of the true Vine; to await the coming of the Son of Man.

A preacher could also specify the function of the homily in relationship to the reign of God in the world. The Scriptures present us with kingdom ideals, a new mode of existence, a different way of seeing the world, a transformed consciousness, improved behavior. When God's reign is operative, justice flows like a mighty stream, the rough ways are made smooth, the lion and the lamb lie down together, Samaritans attend to wounded Jews, blind men see, dying thieves are pardoned, and distraught friends receive the greeting of peace. Some homilies call hearers of the Word to appreciate kingdom ideals, to understand them more deeply, to appropriate their significance, to wrestle with their meaning. Other homilies call for action on behalf of the kingdom—working for justice and peace, bringing forgiveness to family life, healing wounded friendships, taking steps toward greater spiritual maturity. If we make a clear decision to emphasize either a transformation of consciousness or a transformation of behavior, we are in a better position to construct a homily that develops coherently and flows toward a fitting conclusion.

In deciding on a function for our homily, we should consider the various degrees of transformation or conversion we are advocating. Sometimes it seems proper to call for radical transformation, a total change of consciousness, a complete reversal of behavior. A homily based on the Beatitudes in Luke might demand a whole new way of thinking about the poor—what we can learn from them and how we can empower them to take hold of their own lives. In other situations, we might be looking for modification in outlook, a little larger perspective, a modest change in behavior. We might use the cure of the man born blind and his progressive growth in consciousness (John 9:1–41) to call for a well-chosen step forward in overcoming spiritual blindness.

There are many ways of specifying the function of a homily. The important thing is to think through what we are trying to accomplish in a given situation and to arrange the material to achieve this purpose. With focus and function in mind, we can turn to the task of gathering and organizing material for homilies.

KEVIN ANDERSON RESPONSE

In this chapter, Jim gets to the core of his distinctive contribution to preaching theory and practice. His stress on a focus for the homily that emerges from a dialogue between the Scriptures and the human condition is crucial. In our data, the item "This preacher's sermons usually have a clear central message" was a top five predictor of preacher effectiveness. "Central message" is not the same as Jim's concept of focus, but both concepts point to the importance of the preacher being clear on what she or he wants to say. Jim's encouragement that the focus be written down in a single sentence seems like a good discipline for preachers—a test they can use to determine if the listener will hear a clear central message when the homily is delivered.

Jim's emphasis that the homily must also have a function—a transformation of consciousness or behavior—reminds us that preaching is not just about filling out part of the worship service. It is the main place in our culture in which spiritual guidance is offered on the challenges of living and loving as human beings.

Focus

Many times I have found myself angry during homilies because I try to connect with the words but search in vain for anything that seems relevant to my life. Jim is on target when he says that a theme can lose listeners because it may not include shedding light on the path of the listeners' daily lives.

Consider advertisements for automobiles in magazines. Unless you really like cars, you're not likely to pause long to look at these ads. Psychologists would say they are not "salient" to you because many thoughts or concerns are more prominent in your consciousness. This changes, however, when you are in the market for a new car. Suddenly you find yourself actually looking at and reading ads for cars. The ads haven't changed—but they are now relevant to your life.

This is the first challenge of the homilist: to ensure that whatever she or he chooses to speak about addresses a common human concern. Without such salience, the listener's mind will wander as quickly as one could turn to the next page of a magazine.

We chose to call this book *A Light Unto My Path*, not *A Light Unto a Path*. People don't tune in to what a preacher is saying until they decide it can shed some light on their own lives. The human mind does not long attend to generalities that do not appear relevant.

This is the fascinating thing about the data from our studies of preaching. The top two variables to emerge—"keeps my attention" and "knows what is in my heart"—are probably interactive. Keeping listeners' attention is not mainly about telling jokes or using gimmicks; rather, it involves speaking so that listeners feel you know their hearts and can shed light on the joys and struggles they carry inside. When you speak to a relevant human concern that "hits close to home," keeping attention is not a problem. Conversely, when you rivet attention through creative delivery, the listener's heart opens to your message like a flower opens to the morning sun.

I am not a Freudian psychologist, but I frequently share with clients Freud's simple summary of the two pillars of human existence: work and love. If a preacher wants a quick reminder of what is in the hearts of listeners, these two pillars help. "Work," broadly considered, picks up the human concerns of money, success, making ends meet, serving others, unemployment, poverty, and more. "Love" covers most of the rest of life—marriage, sexuality, children, love of God and neighbor, dealing with conflict, and losing loved ones. Today the issue of balancing work and love is also primary in many listeners' minds.

Function

Jim's emphasis that homilies need a function—a call to transformation of consciousness or behavior—made me think of my profession (psychotherapy). Therapists who spend a lot of time talking with clients about how they feel but never get around to discussing concrete changes in thinking or behavior often have clients who stay stuck. Near the end of every therapy session, a little reminder goes off in my head: So we've talked about it, now what can we do about it? The literature on psychotherapy outcomes is clear: simply talking or getting insight into a problem is not usually enough to promote healing and change. I think Jim is saying something parallel about preaching. Relating the Scriptures to a human concern is important, but the additional step of "Now what can we do about it?" is also important.

Behavior change is perhaps the most tangible function of a homily. It would be good if listeners are moved to action by hearing a well-planned and engagingly delivered homily. As a psychologist I would suggest that homilists remember the SAM acronym when making suggestions for behavior change. This acronym reminds us that behavior changes should be:

S: Specific (I will call a soup kitchen to volunteer) instead of general (I should help the poor)

A: Achievable (I will work on behalf of hungry people in my community) versus unachievable (I will figure out how to solve world hunger)

M: Measurable (I will consider volunteering once per month) versus vague (I will volunteer occasionally)

I like Jim's emphasis on transformation in consciousness as another option for the function of the homily. We human beings live in nonconscious ideologies like fish swim in water. This means that we have ways of thinking about the world and our lives that are on automatic pilot and are largely out of our consciousness. When we live on autopilot, we lose awareness of our free will. We begin seeing our subjective truth as objective truth. We need to be awakened when we are asleep, enlightened when we have blind spots. A homily with a clear focus and an invitation to transform our consciousness can do that.

I want to comment on Jim's statement that pastors hear much more about parishioners' difficulties than about their joys. This is also the case in my profession, but people still need a spirituality of joy, an alternative to the culture's false messages that happiness can be found in sex, money, success, or the acquisition of material possessions. Pierre Teilhard de Chardin's statement that "joy is an infallible sign of the presence of God" invites a transformation of consciousness that allows people to begin noticing how God is present in the simple joys of their daily lives.

Focus Leads to Function

If I am reading Jim's material accurately, I sense his approach is something like this:

```
          dialogue                    leads to        leads to
Scripture ◄──────► Human concern ─────────► Focus ─────────► Function
```

When Scripture is held in dialogue with the realities of human existence, a focus for the homily emerges, which pushes us further to ask, "Now what can we do about it?"

JAMES BACIK RESPONSE

Borrowing from Sigmund Freud, Kevin wisely reminds preachers of the importance of work, as well as of love, in human affairs. Many Christians today are indeed looking for guidance in managing the challenges of the world of work. In a recent Labor Day weekend homily, I addressed some of the concerns Kevin associates with work. I began by describing work broadly as all purposeful human activity, including the crucial tasks of raising children and volunteering to serve others and the common good. In a further effort to be inclusive, I noted that some people at Mass had been looking for a job for months without any success, while others have tedious jobs that do not pay a living wage. My focus for the homily was the call of the Gospel (Luke 14:25–33) to keep our priorities straight so that we can surmount the temptation to make an idol out of our work. Many Americans are overworked, spending more time on the job than workers in other industrialized countries. More successful people tend to work longer hours.

To specify the temptations surrounding work I used composite examples: the executive who stepped on people climbing the corporate ladder; the mother who identified herself with raising children and is now overwhelmed by the empty nest syndrome; the workaholic who neglects her family responsibilities; the professor who is envious of the scholarly accomplishments of his colleagues; the student who is hurting her health by working an extra job, an example of the work-and-spend pattern so prevalent in our society. Our culture, which measures success by earning power, reinforces many of the tendencies to turn work into an absolute concern. The Gospel of the day challenges all idol-making by giving the top priority in life to following Christ. Even allowing for Semitic hyperbole (hate your father and mother), the message is radical: discipleship is more important then anything else. The task of spreading the reign of justice and peace deserves our best efforts. A more reliable measure of success is our contribution to the common good. This framework helps keep not only family life, but also our work, in perspective. With the goal of following Christ wholeheartedly, we are in a position to develop a viable spirituality of work. Work is our way of sharing in the creative activity of God and participating in the redemptive work of Christ. Through our work we develop our Spirit-given gifts and talents and are thereby enabled to contribute to the good of others and our world. For disciples of Christ, work takes on a deeper meaning. Work does not define us; it is a gift that enables us to grow spiritually and to make the world a better place.

I then returned to the composite examples, showing how a faith perspective can help all of us manage more effectively the temptations surrounding work. An executive decides to make people more important than success. A mother expands her interests, preparing for the day her children move out. A workaholic decides to spend more time with the family. A teacher becomes less competitive and more satisfied with her own accomplishments. A student cuts back on her hours on the job, spends less money, and devotes more time to study. The conclusion of the homily invited prayerful reflection on ways our work could bring us closer to God. Kevin wants more homilies, not just on Labor Day, that realistically address the many concerns surrounding work, since it occupies so much of our time and energy.

Kevin's point that behavior changes proposed in the homily be specific, achievable, and measurable is well taken. An Ash Wednesday homily calling for prayer, fasting, and almsgiving could be enriched by references to concrete examples of successful efforts in the past. A mother decided to get up a half-hour earlier, before her husband and children awoke, and use the time to reflect on a Scripture passage. She did it almost every day of Lent and found by Easter that she had more energy, was more focused, and functioned better within the family circle. A factory worker adopted the Lenten penance of helping out at a food distribution center once a week. He learned a good deal by interacting with the poor and felt good about helping others, so he decided to continue his weekly service throughout the Easter season. A lawyer decided to use Lent as a time to improve her eating habits. She did not eat between meals, cut down on desserts, and ate small portions. She lost weight, felt better about herself, and has every intention of sticking to her successful regimen. While examples like these can encourage hearers of the Word to make their own Lenten penance specific, achievable, and measurable, I would add this caution: spiritual growth often defies precise measurement, and God works for our good in mysterious ways.

CHAPTER SIX

Composing and Delivering Your Homily

Starting Early

With a specific focus and function clearly in mind, you are prepared to compose your actual homily. It is important to start preparing for the following Sunday early in the week with a period of prayerful reflection. Prayer reminds us of our absolute dependence on God in carrying out the crucial preaching ministry, and it makes us more receptive to the wealth of meaning found in the Scripture passages.

We can think of the composition process as an expansion of the conversation between experience and the biblical text that produced the focus point. This expanded dialogue goes on spontaneously throughout the week in the minds and hearts of preachers as they ponder what they are going to say in the pulpit come Sunday. It is fueled by ministerial experiences and facilitated by the practice of prayerful reflection. These inner conversations seem to have a life of their own, weaving back and forth between existential concerns and Christian teachings. A preacher who simply attends prayerfully to the focus throughout the week sometimes finds elements of the homily spontaneously coming to mind—perhaps a good introductory story, a conversation that exemplifies the concern, a new insight into the Gospel reading, a creative way of relating the concern and the scriptural message, a fitting conclusion.

> A pastor decided to focus on the feminine images of God in Proverbs 8:22–31 as a supplement to the traditional masculine language about God, but had little sense of how to describe the

concern in concrete terms. That week a woman came to him for advice about her inability to pray since her husband had suddenly left her for another woman. She described in vivid detail her anger at men in general and the great anxiety she felt when saying the Lord's Prayer at Mass or praying privately to God the Father. The pastor advised her to reflect on passages in the Bible, such as Proverbs 8, that personify wisdom as a woman so that she could use feminine imagery for God in her prayer life. During the session, the pastor realized that the woman had given him a concrete example of the adverse effects of thinking of God only in male terms. At the end of the session, he asked her if he could use an anonymous version of her story in his homily that Sunday, and she readily agreed. With a prayer of gratitude, he took time between appointments to jot down some notes so he would not forget the colorful phrases the woman used in describing her inability to pray using male imagery.

This story illustrates the importance of deciding on a focus early in the week and listening well to the way individuals express their concerns and insights. If we wait until Friday night to determine the theme of our Sunday homily, we are likely to miss many opportunities to collect valuable homily material.

Effective preachers enrich this informal process of preparation through various structured efforts to gather ideas and compose their homilies. For the sake of analysis, let us break apart an integrated process and consider first the task of filling out the common human concern expressed in the focus point. Scholars who analyze society, culture, and the human psyche can be helpful. A theologian had decided to offer a theological reflection at Mass on Luke 9:18–24, in which Jesus poses the crucial question: "But who do you say I am?" In preparation, he read parts of *American Jesus: How the Son of God Became a National Icon* by Stephen Prothero (New York: Farrar, Straus and Giroux, 2003) and used his models of Jesus as enlightened sage, servant savior, manly redeemer, and superstar to help the congregation understand the cultural influences on their own perception of Jesus. In preparation for a wedding homily, a deacon looked again at Scott Peck's *The Road Less Traveled* (New York: Simon & Schuster, 1978) for his analysis of common perceptions of love in our culture. A pastor preaching on Paul's conviction that the gifts of the Holy

Spirit are given for the common good (1 Cor 12:4–11) used the analysis of individualism in Robert Bellah's *Habits of the Heart* (Berkeley: University of California Press, 1996) to describe the temptations faced by Christians who try to rise above selfishness and serve those in need.

Imaginative literature provides vivid descriptions and striking symbols of the challenges facing human beings in pursuit of Gospel ideals. Homilists have their own favorites to draw on. John Updike's novels deal insightfully with the compelling issues of money, power, sex, and personal relationships. F. Scott Fitzgerald's *Great Gatsby* presents a powerful portrayal of Gatsby's tragic refusal to face reality, a common temptation in the contemporary world as well as in certain biblical stories, such as Peter's misguided attempt to talk Jesus out of the planned journey to Jerusalem (Matt 16:13–23). Often it is not a matter of quoting from a novel or even mentioning it, but of picking up the way the author describes the human scene. For example, Anne Tyler's *Accidental Tourist* (New York: Knopf, 1985) suggests concrete ways in which people sleepwalk through life without really being engaged in its joys and challenges. Homilists who read good fiction have a valuable resource for understanding and describing the human condition.

Movies are also a rich source for filling out the focus point. To take a prime example, the various film versions of Victor Hugo's classic *Les Miserables* provide a vivid portrayal of the conversion of the heroic figure, Jean Valjean, who suffered great injustice and became an instrument of grace for others— a story that exemplifies the teaching of the Sermon on the Mount, especially the injunction to do good to those who persecute us (Matt 5:43–47). The three-volume set *Lights, Camera—Faith* by Peter Malone with Rose Pacatte (Boston: Pauline Books & Media, 2002) offers a summary of a particular movie for all the Sundays of the three-year lectionary cycle. For instance, the authors suggest *Shadowlands* for the fifth Sunday of Easter, Cycle A, presenting the life of C. S. Lewis as an example of the struggle to follow Jesus, who is the way, the truth, and the life (John 14:1–12).

Engaging the Scripture Readings

In this process of gathering material, the preacher must also prayerfully engage the designated Scripture readings. Once again this engagement occurs spontaneously for those who determine a focus point early in the week and keep it in mind. A pastor may remember a verse from the Psalm when visiting the sick. The challenge of the Epistle may trigger an especially self-critical examination of conscience. The main message of the Gospel may be just what a troubled parishioner needs to hear. During meditation, a striking symbol from one of the readings may emerge into consciousness.

An effective homilist finds ways to enrich this spontaneous process. It can be as simple as rereading the passages a couple of times during the week and spending time reflecting on them. Having questions in mind can help you: What image of God is implied? What do the passages teach us about Christ? Which characters intrigue me and why? A homilist reflecting on John 9:1–41 might find him- or herself identifying with the gradual spiritual awakening of the man born blind and, in the process, might come to a deeper appreciation of the mercy of God and the enlightening message of Jesus the master teacher.

Preparation also takes us back to the lectionary commentaries mentioned in chapter 4, which not only help us determine a focus point, but also help fill it out. From them we learn more about the context of each reading, the common themes, the special words, the important symbols, and the relationships among the readings. After pursuing several commentaries on the seventeenth Sunday in Ordinary Time Cycle C (Gen 18:1–10; Col 1:24–28; Luke 10:38–42), a homilist decides to focus on openness and especially hospitality as an antidote to the exclusion of others. One commentary on the gospel story of Martha and Mary suggests that Jesus might be commending Mary for giving personal attention to him as a guest and not being distracted by other duties connected with hospitality. In the story, Jesus himself participates in the open dynamics of hospitality by accepting an invitation from a woman, Martha, to come to her home and by addressing her sister, Mary, as a disciple—both actions in violation of the restrictive customs of the day. From this perspective, the Gospel connects with the first reading, which celebrates the hospitality of Abraham and Sarah and the promise that they would have a child in their old age. The reading from Colossians does not directly relate to the focus point, but it does portray Paul as an example of embracing suffering as a component of following Christ, who suffered for his opposition to rigid religious attitudes and customs.

This example reminds us that the scholarly commentaries on the lectionary readings are especially useful for busy preachers, because they provide us with fresh homily material in a condensed format that can be read rather quickly. Also helpful are the biblical dictionaries—for instance, *The Collegeville Pastoral Dictionary of Biblical Theology*, edited by Carroll Stuhlmueller (Collegeville, MN: Liturgical Press, 1996), which offers concise summaries of biblical themes and traces their historical development and pastoral relevance. A homilist reflecting on Luke's account of the feeding of the multitude (9:10–17) could find, under the theme "meal," an outline of the importance of meals, especially the Passover, in the Hebrew Scriptures; a listing of the seven meals in Luke leading up to the Last Supper, including the multiplying of the loaves; and some general ideas on the symbolic importance of eating together applied to the Eucharist. Even if all of this information does not appear in the homily, it does give the preacher a context for developing the focus.

Literary approaches to the Bible, which draw on semiotics and related fields, guide us in determining the meaning of the scriptural texts and their integrity. This method directs our attention to certain characteristics of the text: the dominant themes, the structure of the text, the frequency of key words, the development of the characters, and the inner dynamics of the passage. From this perspective, a homily on the power of grace to transform takers into givers is exemplified in the encounter between Jesus and Zacchaeus (Luke 19:1–9). Zacchaeus is passionate about finding out what this man Jesus is really like. His efforts are rewarded as he comes to see that Jesus is the Lord, the source of all joyful existence. Zacchaeus, who is a Jew but also a collaborator with the Romans, becomes a true son of Abraham. Formerly he simply collected taxes; now he gives money back to others. Thanks to his encounter with Jesus, he now has a new found joy in his heart.

Sharing in Group Discussions

A preacher can gather valuable homily material by participating in faith-sharing groups that discuss the Sunday readings. In a typical discussion, the prayer at the beginning opens the heart as well as the mind to what the passages meant in the biblical period and what they mean today. A free-flowing discussion will reveal which ideas, verses, images, symbols, and metaphors strike responsive chords with the hearers of the Word. Participants who have read commentaries ahead of time enrich the conversation. Without dominating or controlling the discussion, the homilist can usually elicit responses to his intended focus point by raising it explicitly or posing appropriate questions. Parishioners generally appreciate being included in this phase of homily preparation. By listening well to them, a pastor can learn more about the actual meaning of a particular Scripture passage for people today. When someone makes an especially insightful comment or shares a relevant story, the pastor can ask permission to use it or note that an anonymous version might appear in the homily.

Some pastors discuss the Sunday readings with members of their staff each week. If everyone reads a different commentary in preparation, the discussion can generate many useful ideas drawn from biblical scholars and filtered through the experience of individuals who serve the church. Such discussions could be used to generate a focus point. If the homilist has already determined the focus, then the staff members can frame their comments around it. This process not only helps the pastor gather homily material; it also draws the staff together around the biblical Word proclaimed in worship.

Preachers who meet regularly with their colleagues from other Christian denominations for ecumenical discussions of the common lectionary report that over time they learn to recognize different perspectives and nuances in the readings that enrich their homily preparation. A Catholic participant, for example, might gain a greater appreciation of the Protestant perspective on the theme of grace alone in Paul's letters. Doing homily preparation with denominational colleagues can also surface fresh ideas, especially since individual homilists tend to view the Scriptures through their own theological lens and the dominant concerns of their congregations. A suburban pastor could preach more effectively on social justice after dialogue with central city pastors, who read the Scriptures with the needs of the poor in mind.

All preachers who take the time to participate in a discussion of the Sunday readings with any group benefit not only from what others contribute but also from the opportunity to experiment with initial articulations of the points percolating in their own hearts and minds.

At some point in the week, we must compose our homily out of all the material we have gathered. Most effective preachers actually sit down and write out an outline, or notes, or a complete text. As with all phases of the preparation process, veteran preachers have their own habitual, often unexamined, way of doing this.

A busy pastor decided on Monday to focus on the contemporary problem of doubt in the light of the encounter between the risen Christ and Thomas in John 20:24–29. During the week he read a commentary that pointed out that Thomas at first felt isolated from the other disciples, who were so ecstatic about seeing the Lord; but after his own encounter with the risen Lord, he made a great profession of faith that reestablished his solidarity with his fellow disciples.

At his regular Bible study with a small group of parishioners, the pastor asked them to share some of their doubts about faith and how they coped with them. One young widow told a graphic story of how she came to doubt God's love after the untimely death of her husband. Recognizing that the story fit well with the sermon focus, he secured permission to use the story without mentioning her name. Friday afternoon he went to his computer and typed out an outline of his sermon. He began the body of the homily, as usual, with a description of the doubt of Thomas and of his great expression of faith. He then pointed out that Christ was talking about us when he said: Blessed are those who have not seen and have believed (John 20:29). With that transition, he then applied the Gospel lesson by telling the story of the widow, including the way she came again to believe in God's love of her. After getting the body of the homily in order, he added an introduction that set a context by explaining that John's Gospel highlights various encounters between Jesus and specific individuals like Thomas, and a conclusion that invited the congregation to reflect on the message of the Gospel.

Like the homilist in the example, most preachers have their favorite, often unreflected, ways of organizing their material and composing their homilies. We can all find ways of improving our preaching by explicitly considering specific questions about the components and dynamics of this process. How can we describe the focus in ways that draw in more hearers of the Word? What function do stories have, and how should we use them? What is the best order and sequence for relating common human experience and the scriptural passages? What is the function of the introduction? How does the conclusion relate to the purpose of the homily?

Describing the Focus Point

Good descriptions that exemplify the focus point and resonate with the congregation are crucial to homily effectiveness. We need to describe the common human experiences of joy and sorrow, success and failure, virtue and vice, good and evil in ways that draw the congregation into the dynamics of the focus. We want those who listen to the homily to identify with the description, to see themselves in the portrayal of the human adventure. Typical comments by parishioners to good preachers reveal this resonance. "Your homily spoke to my heart." "I don't know how you know so much about my inner struggles." "You said clearly what I have felt vaguely." "That story was about me." "You must have been listening to our family discussions."

The psychologist Abraham Maslow found that when he described peak experiences to people in abstract terms, such as being peaceful or integrated, very few would claim to have such experiences. If, however, he read them a report of an actual peak experience expressed in striking imagery and colorful language ("rhapsodizing," he called it), many more people would recognize that something similar had happened to them. A homilist with a poetic soul has the ability to use rhapsodic language in describing the depth experiences of life. Those of us who lack that gift can often find striking imagery in the Scripture readings that can also touch the imagination. The psalms in the common lectionary are filled with poetic language. The righteous are "like trees planted by streams of water," while the wicked are "like chaff that the wind drives away" (Ps 1:1–6). Our God is "slow to anger and abounding in steadfast love," like "a father who has compassion for his children" (Ps 103:1–13). The psalms, which are an important part of the common lectionary, are filled with metaphors, images, and colorful descriptions of a wide variety of human emotions that can stir the imagination and touch the heart.

Learning from Ordinary People

Much of the valuable descriptive material in homilies comes from common human experience expressed in homey ways by ordinary people. A mother of three youngsters says wryly that if she doesn't get more help from her husband, she is going "to resign and forfeit being mother of the year." A successful executive declares that what "gives him the deepest sense of satisfaction" is that his teenage son still talks to him about personal issues. A mother dying of cancer, who desperately wants to be a good example to her husband and children, pleads with her pastor: "Don't let me mess this up." A single woman who quit a successful career in the corporate world to work for the church attributed her "new and exciting sense of purpose in life" to a homily on the gospel call to discipleship. Good pastors listen well to the ways their parishioners speak about the human adventure, and they quote those lines back to them in their homilies.

Sometimes a preacher picks up the general sense of what people are feeling about the struggles and joys of human relationships. A homilist who does a good deal of counseling draws on his experience to describe some of the challenges built into the commandment to love our neighbor: love raises high expectations that can never be totally fulfilled; sooner or later we disappoint our loved ones just as they disappoint us; individuals are sometimes too preoccupied with their own problems to listen to their friends; at times spouses are not really present when their partners need them. Parishioners who hear this kind of description sense that the preacher knows their heart, and they are thus disposed to listen to the rest of the story.

Back to the example: The preacher then noted some comments of parishioners that suggest that following the example and command of Jesus can bring a renewed sense of fulfillment and enlightenment. "When we make love after an argument, I feel accepted and treasured." "When I apologized to my friend, I did not feel particularly good about it, but I knew it was the Christian thing to do." "Taking food to my sick neighbor on a regular basis has helped me handle my depression better." Positive examples of this kind not only manifest the power of grace active in the lives of others but also serve as an invitation to all the members of the congregation to go and do likewise.

The Homilist's Own Experience

The way preachers choose and interpret the descriptive material in a homily will always reflect their own interests. Sometimes a preacher draws very explicitly on his or her own personal experiences. For example, a Protestant minister who does not follow the common lectionary announced to the congregation that he was going to preach a series of six sermons on his personal struggles to live as a Christian in the contemporary world. Attendance went up week by week and the feedback multiplied, indicating generally positive responses to his personal witness. Caution is certainly needed in using personal experiences. The pulpit is not a confessional. A steady diet of very personal material can draw more attention to the preacher than to the message. It also can put more emphasis on churchy concerns than on life in the world as most Christians know it.

Carl Jung, the psychotherapist who has influenced important spiritual writers such as John Sanford and Morton Kelsey, wisely taught that with the great questions of life, it is enough to have wrestled with them. It is crucial that homilists wrestle with the great issues of meaning, purpose, identity, relationships, freedom, God, Christ, revelation, justice, death, and afterlife. We do not need to pretend that we have definitive answers to the great questions, but our homilies should suggest that we have struggled with their complexity and are aware of the wisdom of the Christian tradition in dealing with them. This is a more subtle way of drawing on our own experience in composing our homilies. Following this approach, a homilist would not directly mention her own personal doubts about her faith but would describe the common struggles with belief in the contemporary world in such a way that people in the congregation would recognize that she knows the same temptations that they do. Our credibility suffers if we give the impression that we have pat, easy answers to vexing questions. Preachers who personally engage the focus point throughout the week are more likely to reflect their own experience in the homily, even if they choose not to make explicit reference to themselves. This more subtle method wears better over the long haul than constant personal references.

Learning from Phenomenology

Insights from the field of phenomenology, associated with influential philosophers such as Edmund Husserl, Martin Heidegger, and Paul Ricoeur, can improve our efforts to fill out the focus point with descriptive material. The phenomenologists are interested in describing human experience accurately while bracketing the question of truth claims. Edmund Husserl (1859–1938), the founder of phenomenology, reminds us to include in our homilies descriptions of the dynamics of consciousness. For example, a homily focused on the claim of Jesus to bring refreshment and rest to weary souls (Matt 11:25–30) might describe the insatiable desire for the perfect lover, our deep longing for someone who will fulfill all our needs, a person who will hold us when we are sad and laugh with us when we are joyful. Our fundamental inability to satisfy this thirst for a completely satisfying human love raises the question whether we are really a useless passion, as Jean-Paul Sartre claimed, or whether there is validity in the promise of Christ to give rest to our souls. Perhaps we can detect clues in ordinary life that there is indeed a final fulfillment of this longing for perfect love—a moment of prayer when we rested comfortably in Christ or a charitable deed that created bonds of solidarity with someone in need and with the Christ who identifies with them. As a homilist, you can tap the great interest in spirituality today by including wide-ranging descriptions of the various ways people are searching for deeper meaning, purpose, and relational identity.

Martin Heidegger (1889–1976), a student of Husserl and commonly recognized as a leading existentialist philosopher, directs our attention to "our being in the world," the ways that we, as total persons, actually live in our particular life situations and social settings. We are "thrown into existence" and find ourselves embedded in a whole network of relationships. Homilies that describe well various ways of being in the world help hearers of the Word understand the challenges and opportunities of living as Christians in our cultural matrix and societal setting. We can imagine a homily on the challenging call to discipleship (Luke 10:1–20) that uses personal examples of life situations familiar to a particular congregation. A small business owner with a tight budget and large family to support struggles with his Christian responsibility to pay his employees a fair wage. A mother of three who feels like a taxi driver chauffeuring her kids to all their activities is searching for a gospel spirituality that will give her a deeper sense of purpose in life. A single mother on welfare, caught in the hellish circle of poverty with no health insurance, wonders how she can be a better role model for her teenage daughter. A lawyer who enjoys a luxurious lifestyle decides to devote himself to serving the common good by helping those in need. Such descriptions are helpful in giving the focus point a concrete context.

The philosopher Paul Ricoeur, who encouraged us in chapter 4 to find the meaning in front of Scripture texts, teaches us the importance of symbols in understanding and describing human experience. Symbols shape our imagination and influence how we see the world. Symbols give rise to thought, as Ricoeur insists, and gather together diverse experiences and ideas. Hearers of the Word are more likely to remember and appreciate the message of the homily when it is held together by a clear symbol. Jesus used the image of the kingdom to exemplify important elements of his teaching.

A homilist can often find useful symbols in the Scripture readings. For example, a homily focused on the temptation to evade the command of Jesus to take up our cross could use the story of Jonah, who unsuccessfully tried to escape his obligation to preach repentance to the Ninevites. Jonah symbolizes all ill-advised efforts to escape the cross of daily discipleship: drinking, drugs, utopian thinking, undisciplined lifestyle, procrastination. The Jonah syndrome is common, and the image of Jonah, drawn from a well-known story, is easily remembered. It invites all of us to reflect on our own escapist tendencies and on the wisdom of following the will of God by taking up the cross daily. As homilists we should always be on the lookout for striking symbols that grab the attention of our parishioners and linger in their minds and hearts.

In summary, the field of phenomenology encourages preachers to keep in mind their parishioners' conscious interests and intentions, their various life situations, and their need for symbols that are easily remembered and prompt further reflection.

Inclusive Descriptions

When you preach, you will want to draw as many of the hearers of the Word as possible into the dynamic of your homily. Not every group can be mentioned in a given sermon. Over a period of time, however, our examples should include men and women, young and old, married and single, and persons with a heterosexual and a homosexual orientation. We should try to imagine the ways various people experience the concern and live out the scriptural message. In a homily focused on the challenge of helping those in need (Matt 25:31–46), you might note the common excuses: I've got my own problems and can't be worried about all those poor people; I can't even think about all the starving people in the world because it tears me up; what can I possibly do about such great problems; in the past I tried to help the homeless but the problem is just too massive; we don't have much ourselves, how can we be expected to help others; some of those people on welfare don't work and drive expensive cars. Other believers have seen Christ in the needy and have found ways to help: a family joined Bread for the World; a single woman tutors inner-city children; a group of collegians makes pizzas and distributes them to the hungry; a lawyer increased her pro bono work for the poor; a doctor went to Guatemala for a month to offer free medical care; a single man who was unemployed for years and recently found a job is helping some of his friends on welfare find work. Our descriptions should reflect both the existential concern and the power of the gospel to transform lives.

Another way of helping people identify with the focus point is to use language that appeals to various groups. One obvious example is to attend to gender issues: sometimes engineers should be women and single parents should be fathers. Another less obvious point is that individuals process information in diverse ways: some people see things while others hear or feel them. Thus, in talking about God's revelation in history, we might encourage people to be watchful for intimations of the divine presence; to listen carefully to the whisperings of the Spirit; and to feel the warm presence of the risen Christ. Homilists who listen well and are open to critical comments will gradually learn which groups they tend to exclude and ways of drawing more people into the challenge and response summarized in the focus point.

Use of Stories

Stories that elaborate the focus and promote the specific function are important to homily effectiveness and deserve special attention. The narrative theology that developed in a North American context during the last third of the twentieth century helps us understand the importance and the limitations of stories in preaching. Human beings are historical creatures. By our daily decisions, we author a story that can be examined for its consistency and appropriateness. In our personal history, we meet God and hear the divine message. The Bible, the normative witness to God's revelation, has a narrative structure that places the divine Word in a historical context. Christ, the definitive prophet and master teacher, made use of parables to teach the truth of the kingdom and to draw disciples into the task of spreading God's reign. The gospels place the saving work of Jesus and his fundamental teachings in the framework of a story that, in its broadest dimensions, moves through his preexistence as the Eternal Word, his conception, birth, public life, arrest, execution, resurrection, and ascension to the right hand of God. From this perspective, narrative precedes doctrine and dogma as the primary vehicle of revelation. The biblical stories are not merely illustrations of moral admonitions and doctrinal truths, but are themselves vehicles of divine revelation. They keep alive the memory of God's mighty deeds and the saving work of Christ. The classic stories of the saints remind us of the ways people throughout history have lived out Christian discipleship. Contemporary stories that illumine the depth dimensions of the human adventure can be used to show how God continues to be active in the world today.

Narrative Theology

Narrative theology sets the framework for further reflection on the use of stories in homilies. Because both human existence and biblical revelation have a narrative structure, stories can find a natural home in homilies. Not only do they gain attention—they also convey divine truth. Narrative preaching speaks to the whole person, heart as well as mind. Stories touch the imagination and linger in the memory. They have an inherent power to command attention and to maintain interest. They enhance the power of images, symbols, metaphors, and analogies to illumine the human condition by placing them in a narrative context. The great foundational stories, known as myths, help us understand our deepest relationships to God, others, and the world. Shared stories bind us together in a community of faith and link us to ages of Christians past and future. Personal narratives that reflect the paschal mystery of Jesus provide us with concrete examples of the power of divine grace to transform death into life.

At an even more fundamental level, the very act of preaching has a narrative structure. As a homilist you have the task of linking the biblical stories with contemporary stories of faith. Preaching is an event—it creates an encounter between God's Word and human beings with questioning hearts. Effective homilies often sound more like an unfolding story than the development of a logical outline. They create a sense of movement, tension, ambiguity, and expectancy rather than relying on clear, fixed, static conclusions. Effective narrative preaching leads the congregation into the dramatic story of God's ongoing love for the human family.

An effective homilist will choose stories that exemplify the focus, contribute to the function or goal, and speak to the congregation. These criteria rule out some narrative types: for example, tales, even gripping ones, that have no connection with the existential concern or the scriptural message; humorous stories, even very funny ones, that have nothing to do with the personal conversion or transformed world envisioned in the homily; celebrity stories, even interesting ones, that do not resonate with the experience of the congregation; personal stories of the preacher that detract from the function of the homily; stories about parishioners that would reveal their identity or embarrass them; any narrative that breaks confidentiality or would be considered out of line by reasonable parishioners.

When we preach, we need ways to make the biblical narratives come alive for people today. When the readings are proclaimed with prayerful respect and clear meaning, they have an inherent power to touch the minds and hearts of the congregation. Generally, parishioners report that they do not want the homily to repeat the readings in the same words—yet the homilists can help people hear the passages in a fresh way by retelling them in more popular language or in a different setting or from a different perspective. A preacher could tell the story of Jesus visiting Mary and Martha's home from the viewpoint of Lazarus, their brother, who tries to reconcile the two approaches to hospitality. We could imagine John the Baptist delivering his harsh Advent condemnations in a shopping mall during the Christmas season, carefully choosing the contemporary vernacular for "you brood of vipers" (Matt 3:7).

Sometimes it is helpful to point out relevant details in the story. For instance, Luke introduces the story of the Good Samaritan with the scholar's question, admittedly disingenuous, asking what he must do to gain eternal life, and concludes it with Jesus telling him to follow the example of the Samaritan—details that suggest that this memorable parable is really an example story demonstrating how to live a fulfilling life and not merely an answer to a theoretical question. Preachers who recognize that the Bible stories are normative but culturally conditioned vehicles of divine truth will feel free to search for creative ways to express their literal meaning and fuller sense.

Stories of the Saints

The classic stories of great Christian disciples are an almost unlimited, if generally untapped, resource for homiletic material: the conversion of Augustine, the preaching ministry of Hildegard of Bingen, the vocation choice of Aquinas, the reforming zeal of Luther, the spiritual journey of Teresa of Avila, the courageous decision of Thomas More. The spiritual insights of modern authors such as Thérèse of Lisieux, Thomas Merton, Dietrich Bonhoeffer, and Dorothy Day carry greater weight when rooted in their personal stories. A preacher with a strong sense of God's will to save all people and the universality of grace can make use of inspiring stories from outside the Christian tradition. To take just one example, the autobiography of Mohandas Gandhi, *The Story of My Experiments with Truth* (Boston: Beacon Press, 1957), contains powerful stories that exemplify particular Christian values, such as nonviolence and asceticism.

Stories of Ordinary People

Contemporary stories of ordinary people struggling to live out the gospel in everyday circumstances sometimes provide some of the most compelling homiletic material. The effective homilist is on the alert for such stories as they surface in the course of daily ministry.

A pastor had decided to focus on the struggle between spirit and flesh in the quest for genuine Christian freedom as portrayed by Paul in Galatians 5:1, 13–18. During his week of preparation, a happily married woman and mother of a month-old gift-from-God infant came to him asking for spiritual guidance. Twice before in her life she had been diagnosed with breast cancer and had undergone apparently successful operations and chemotherapy. Now she had just been diagnosed with liver cancer. She was prepared for the physical sufferings ahead of her and dismissed them as quite manageable. Her real pain was emotional and psychological as she contemplated the burden on her husband and the possibility that her daughter would grow up without ever knowing her. She fully intended to fight this cancer as she had the others and, as a woman of deep faith, to continue to seek God's help. Her real temptation, as she described it, was to feel sorry for herself, to act like a victim, to wallow in self-pity. She feared that her illness would come to define her. There was another part of her, the faith-filled part, that knew a deeper truth about herself: that she was first of all a child of God, a disciple of Christ, blessed in so many ways, especially with a child she never expected to have. Realizing that the inner struggle to define herself properly was crucial to the way she handled this latest cross, she was looking for advice on how to maintain a faith-inspired perspective.

Recognizing the spiritual maturity of the woman, the pastor encouraged her to continue the spiritual exercises that got her through her two previous bouts with cancer: daily prayer and meditation, a conscious effort to accept God's will, and a commitment to do good for others, especially her husband. He also suggested she tell her many concerned relatives and friends that she wanted prayers from them and not pity, which would only fuel her temptation to feel sorry for herself. Awestruck by her remarkable courage and deep faith, the pastor concluded with a tearful prayer beseeching the healing Spirit to be with her during this most trying time.

The next day, while praying, the pastor realized that the woman's story was an amazingly apt example of the struggle between the spirit and the flesh described by Paul. He called her and asked permission to use her story slightly disguised in his homily that Sunday. She readily agreed and thanked him for honoring her very personal story in a way that could help others.

This is an amazingly poignant and fitting demonstration of the power of narrative to illumine the struggles of life and the wisdom of the gospel. Preachers who have a focus in mind and listen well are more likely to come up with real-life stories that can inspire and guide others.

Use of Personal Stories

As we have noted previously in a couple of places, special problems can arise with stories that include the homilist as one of the characters. Such personal stories run the danger of focusing on the preacher rather than on the scriptural message. In the worst cases, preaching becomes an ego trip rather than a proclamation of the Word of God. Stories that feature the preacher's ministerial successes, exciting vacations, influential friends, or worldly connections are generally annoying and probably account for the current reaction of some parishioners and scholars against narrative preaching. Keeping ourselves out of the story can reduce the danger of distorting the message. When telling the story about the woman fighting a third cancer, I deliberately did not include myself in it so as to highlight her courage and not my pastoral advice. By introducing stories as disguised or composite, we gain greater freedom to write ourselves out of them, if that seems appropriate.

On the other hand, stories of the preacher can be effective instruments of communicating the gospel. The apostle Paul used both his own striking religious experiences and his tale of sufferings to preach Jesus Christ crucified and risen. Throughout history, great saints such as Augustine of Hippo and Thérèse of Lisieux have used personal narrations to exemplify the power of divine grace at work in their lives. In recent years, many homilists have improved their preaching by employing personal stories instead of relying solely on logical applications of Scripture texts and church doctrines. Homilies that reveal the preacher's failures or struggles can encourage others to deal better with their own challenges.

In deciding whether to use a particular personal story, we should ask if it exemplifies the focus point and contributes to the function of the homily. Does the story of the preacher highlight the Gospel message or overshadow it? Does it help the congregation experience the call to personal conversion and societal transformation? Does the story give fitting witness to the power of God's grace in the life of the homilist? Will the story draw the congregation into the dynamics of the focus point or direct their attention to the person of the preacher? Will the personal story help connect the biblical narrative with the stories of the hearer of the Word? The answers to these questions will depend, in part, on the general relationship between the pastor and the parishioners as well as on the preacher's skills in telling personal stories. Over time, some homilists find that they can trust their intuition to make good decisions about personal material. Others should approach the issue more reflectively by considering these questions and seeking feedback from honest critics.

Sequence

Once we have filled out the focus point with carefully chosen descriptions, examples, images, and stories, we have the task of finding the best sequence for relating the existential concern and Scripture message. All homilists do this automatically, and many have a standard method that they follow. The most common approach is to explain the Scripture passages and then apply them to the needs and challenges of the congregation. Another simple method is to describe the various aspects of the concern and then show how the Scriptures respond with guidance and encouragement. A conscious, purposeful choice of a fitting sequence can improve the flow and effectiveness of a homily. A preacher who accepts a mutually critical method of correlation is free to look for the most fitting and effective sequence of movement between common experience and the Christian message. A pastor who habitually begins with explanations of the Scripture passages runs the danger of losing the attention of parishioners, who are more interested in practical applications to their lives today than in what happened back there in the biblical period.

Periodically reversing the sequence by beginning with a description of contemporary challenges and concerns can gain the attention of the congregation. A homilist who always begins with the existential concern, however, can easily allow long stories or detailed descriptions to dominate the Scripture passages. Sometimes we best achieve the purpose of our homily by retelling the biblical stories first and then sharing how they illumine and guide the common human adventure in its various distinctive modes.

The homilist who is aware of the importance of sequence can find more creative ways of moving between experience and Scripture. In my homily on Christian freedom and the struggle between flesh and spirit (Gal 5:1, 13–18), I allowed the flow of the story of the mother (I called her Esther) battling a third cancer to direct the sequence. Paul gives us an abstract teaching on freedom, but the story of Esther makes it concrete. She is struggling with the flesh, the temptation to question God, to act like a victim, and to define herself as a sick person. This is one version of Paul's notion of the flesh, all those forces that take us away from God and make us selfish. Esther and Paul move us to examine how we define ourselves according to the flesh. Some people tend to define themselves negatively: I am a victim, a loser, an addict, a divorcee. Others view themselves in terms of achievement and success: I am rich, famous, powerful, respected, virtuous. Like Esther, we should all examine how we define ourselves. Note that the sequence is experience, Scripture, application.

I then went on with Esther's story. In her great faith she knows she is a child of God, saved by Christ, blessed by the Spirit. She is the one who has a loving husband and a beautiful child. She defeated cancer twice and wants to maintain hope that she can do it again. All of this is what Paul means by spirit. Esther and Paul remind us that we are more than our successes and failures. We are defined by our relationship to the one God. Once again the sequence is Esther's story, Paul's teaching, and an application to us.

Following the same pattern, the final part of the body of the homily began by describing Esther's plan to avoid self-pity through prayer and concrete acts of charity, precisely the strategy advocated by Paul and one that will help all of us experience the freedom promised by Christ.

In this example, the inner logic of Esther's inspiring story determined the overall development of the homily as well as the order within each section. We could imagine other ways of relating

Esther's story and Paul's teaching. The homilist who thinks through the question of sequence rather than just automatically following a familiar pattern is more likely to draw people into the dynamics of the focus point and achieve the purpose of the homily.

Introductions

After filling out the focus and deciding on the sequence, the preacher must carefully craft an introduction that gains or keeps the initial attention of the congregation and leads into the next part of the homily. The introduction should draw attention to some aspect of the focus point. Generally, it should not include humorous anecdotes or interesting stories that have no connection with the focus point. The preacher should remember that some members of the congregation have just listened attentively to the Scripture readings and probably do not want to hear a simple repetition.

Effective introductions draw the congregation into the conversation between experience and Scripture that has already taken place in the mind and heart of the preacher. The homilist can invite people into this conversation by beginning with experience or with Scripture. He or she can begin with a good story, an insightful question, a summary quote, a provocative statement, or, from the Scripture side, with a creative retelling of the biblical story, an intriguing image from the readings, a key verse, or a fresh perspective on the essence of the message. Some examples suggest the possibilities. A homily for the Thirtieth Sunday in Ordinary Time Cycle C, which includes the boasting of Paul in 2 Timothy 4:6–18 and that of the Pharisee in Luke 18:9–14, began with the question: "Why do we say Paul is humble and the Pharisee is not, although both are boasting in the readings we just heard?" A preacher could begin his homily on Christ's promise to give us peace in the midst of the crosses of life (John 14:25–31) with the story of Cardinal Joseph Bernardin's embrace of death as a friend, which brought him the great gift of peace in his final days. In exploring various meanings of the pronouncement of Jesus that his disciples travel lightly (Mark 6:6–13), a homilist might start with an adaptation of a popular Buddhist story. After years of training, two monks set out to preach the gospel, carrying only the bare essentials for survival. Along the way, they meet a beautiful young woman who needs help to cross a stream. The one monk picks her up, carries her across the water, and sets her down on the other side. About two hours later, the other monk berates him for having such close physical contact with a woman. The first monk responded: "Yes, I did pick her up, but then I set her down. You are still carrying her in your head." Effective preachers find creative introductions that draw hearers of the Word into the dynamics of the focus point.

Conclusions

The conclusion should reflect the function of the homily and not raise new issues or convey new information. At the end of long homilies people do not want extended conclusions. Effective conclusions invite people to apply the message in some way. A preacher might conclude her sermon on recognizing our dependence on God in a culture of self-assertion with a prayer to God the source of all blessings. A homily on the demands of social justice could end with a period of reflection on the possibilities for action written out in the bulletin. A homilist who put forth Thomas the Apostle as an example of the triumph of faith over doubt could bring the reflection to a fitting close by repeating the great faith statement of Thomas: "My Lord and my God." A homily designed to promote charity among dissenting groups in the church could end with the invitation to discuss the main point with a person sitting next to you. Some homilies are strengthened by a comprehensive summary that pulls together the major points. Sometimes a question posed for a moment of reflection can help achieve the transformation of consciousness envisioned by the homily. The homily that concludes appropriately is more likely to end on a consistent note that sticks with the assembly.

Prophetic Preaching

Prophetic preaching, which addresses social, political, and economic issues, poses special difficulties for the homilist. In many situations, pastors can anticipate negative reactions from parishioners to homilies that deal with justice and peace issues. Those who think that religion is a private matter may get angry that questions of public policy are even brought up from the pulpit. The affluent may feel guilty when preachers describe the plight of the poor. Those on the margins may be disappointed that the call to work for justice is too weak. The apathetic may be disturbed by calls to fight injustice. Homilies on controversial issues of peace and war can split a congregation or move people to leave the church. Pastors who have encountered disgruntled parishioners upset with their prophetic preaching can attest to the intensity of these negative reactions.

The complex character of many political, economic, and social issues sharpens the challenge for preachers. It takes extra time and study to understand these issues and the controversies surrounding them. In some cases, a preacher must address legitimate disagreements among Christians of good will. Some homilists feel intimidated by individuals in the congregation who know more about a specific social issue than they do.

Despite all these difficulties, we have a responsibility to preach the gospel of Jesus Christ in such a way that can never be confined to what is safe, comforting, and private. Although Jesus did not produce a detailed program for transforming political and social structures, his teachings on love of neighbor, forgiveness, renunciation of power, and equality of all persons have implications for the way we organize society and treat the less fortunate. Jesus worked for the cause of the God who delivered the Israelites from the cruel fate of slaves and gave them political, economic, and social freedom. Following the great Hebrew prophets, he came to free the captives and to preach the good news to the poor. He identified himself with the hungry and the homeless. Preaching that is faithful to the memory of Jesus must be prophetic—it must attend to the implications of the gospel in the public forum.

Theology buttresses this scriptural imperative. We are socially interdependent creatures, members of the one human family, who bear responsibility for the well-being of our brothers and sisters in Christ. Our God, who loves all human beings, has special care for widows, orphans, and aliens. God's self-giving love redeems the whole world and all aspects of human existence, including the social and institutional dimensions. The divine presence is revealed in the struggle to establish the reign of justice and peace in the world. The risen Christ uses us as instruments to carry on his liberating work in the world. The church has the task of keeping alive the challenging as well as the comforting message of Jesus. The liturgical life of the church encourages and nourishes members for the crucial task of humanizing the world. There is an essential unity between love of God and love of neighbor, just as there is a fundamental deceit in separating them. Love of neighbor must take into account social sin and the false consciousness it generates. Institutions can be unjust and social systems can oppress groups without good people even recognizing it.

Our Christian faith calls us to both personal conversion and social transformation, to put on the mind of Christ and to spread the reign of justice and peace in the world. Genuine discipleship includes good citizenship. Joining the struggle against injustice and violence is an essential component of preaching the gospel. Solidarity with the poor and oppressed gives credibility to the proclamation of God's saving and liberating love. As these brief summary statements suggest, theology provides solid reasons for preaching on social issues, despite the apathy and anger of some parishioners.

Prophetic preaching cannot be an exercise in partisan politics. In the United States, it is neither legitimate nor fitting to use the pulpit to support a certain candidate for office. A homilist should not pretend that a particular public policy option has the force of dogma or is the only alternative when people of good will have honest disagreements on the issue. Prophetic homilies do have the important function of providing a moral framework for analyzing social issues and making judgments about the best options. Many parishioners do need encouragement from the pulpit to bring their faith to the public forum: to vote and do so intelligently; to participate in civic life; to study the issues; to work for justice and peace; to join a voluntary association that works for the common good; to give concrete assistance to people in need. At the same time, those who are already involved as good citizens need a message of hope that their efforts are not in vain, that despite frequent defeats, the good will finally triumph over all the demonic forces. The effective homilist helps individuals form their conscience so that they can make good judgments about social, political, and economic polices that respect the inherent dignity of persons and promote the common good. Such a preacher encourages dialogue on the problems and collaboration on solving them. Good preaching on social issues draws people into the liberating work of Christ, who identifies himself with those in need.

Prophetic preaching is clearly an art, and effective homilists find creative ways of proclaiming the liberating power of the gospel. We should take on the task with a modest confidence that our Christian tradition has something important to say about social issues without claiming to have all the answers to complex problems. Prayerful reflection reminds us of crucial truths: we are empowered by the Holy Spirit, who can strengthen weak homilists; and we stand, along with the assembly, under the judgment of the gospel. Cooperating with the Spirit, we can help build our confidence by learning as much as we can in a short time about a specific issue. Organizations like Bread for the World and Network provide brief reports on current social topics. Consulting with an expert in our parish on a specific homily focus can help us proclaim the prophetic Word with greater confidence and less fear of factual errors in describing the social concern.

Preaching on political and economic questions is strengthened when it is part of a larger parish effort to raise consciousness on social issues and to promote justice and peace in concrete ways. In one sense, all preaching has a prophetic dimension. A pastor who regularly uses examples that demonstrate the call to social transformation as well as personal conversion has prepared the congregation for a homily focused on a specific problem. Preaching on the biblical mandate to care for the poor is more credible and forceful in a parish that runs a food distribution program for hungry people in the area.

When we preach, we should carefully and explicitly distinguish between clear biblical teaching and universal ethical principles, on the one hand, and, on the other, specific policies and proposals that generate disagreement among people of good will. While it is fitting and proper to proclaim that Jesus identified himself with the homeless and that Christians have an obligation to help shelter people, it would be wrong and inappropriate to insist that one of a number of legitimate housing policy options is the only Christian solution. Furthermore, a preacher must respect the integrity of the Scripture passages that reflect a social context and cultural milieu far different from our own. The Bible does not envision modern economies or nuclear weapons. The admonition of Jesus to render to Caesar what is Caesar's does not tell us which tax policy best serves all the citizens of the United States today. Nevertheless, the Hebrew Scriptures and the teachings of Jesus have social ramifications that a preacher can highlight. The story of the rich young man who goes away sad after Jesus invites him to give his wealth to the poor and follow him legitimately suggests a call to the well-off to follow Christ by finding ways to empower the poor to take hold of their own lives.

A homily that encourages concrete efforts to promote justice and peace should provide some options for action; otherwise people become frustrated or end up feeling guilty. In the homily on helping the poor, the pastor could list some options: join Bread for the World, which lobbies Congress for legislation to help feed the hungry; contribute to the Catholic Campaign for Human Development, which offers the poor not a handout but a way out; help out at a food distribution center, which puts you in contact with poor individuals; read a book or article on the root causes of poverty; serve as a big brother or big sister to an impoverished youngster; provide professional assistance to a needy family; pray regularly for the unemployed. By involving parishioners in creating a list of options for specific action, pastors can multiply the positive effects of the homily. Options could include activities that involve personal encounters, use of professional expertise, and efforts to transform systems.

Stories that illustrate the focus point can be an inspiring and nonthreatening way to draw people into the dynamics of a prophetic homily. Stories have the advantage of suggesting concrete ways in which real people struggle with social sin and respond to God's grace. Jesus used parables to prod people into considering alternative ways of understanding and organizing human affairs.

In one parish, a number of parishioners were involved in a hands-on effort to help three homeless, unemployed African American women (mother, daughter, and niece) break out of poverty and move into the mainstream of American life. After years of persistent hard work by all concerned, the daughter, who already had a college degree, finally secured a full-time teaching job that enabled the women to afford their own apartment. In a homily, the pastor simply told the story of the three women: living on the street or in shelters, unable to bathe before job interviews, no car to get around, no phone to check on employment opportunities, waiting in line for welfare assistance, unable to get food stamps. He also noted the parishioners who got them a trailer to live in, drove them to job interviews, found them clothes, stood with them in lines, helped them through the bureaucratic maze of the welfare system, got the niece into school, took them shopping, gave them money, and offered prayerful encouragement when prospects looked the worst. The story gave the congregation some inkling of what it is like to be poor in the United States today. It challenged those who think everyone on welfare is lazy and uneducated. The story also encouraged parishioners to find their own ways to practice the law of love of neighbor in concrete ways.

Effective prophetic homilies get people to think about important issues. While the question of invading Iraq was being debated nationally, a priest began his homily by recognizing that people in the congregation had very different views on the wisdom of going to war. Rather than taking sides, he challenged the assembly to think through how they arrived at their position, and he gave some possible examples. Saddam Hussein is a cruel dictator, and we should use our military might to remove him. Jesus taught nonviolence, and therefore I am against all war. We have to go to war or the United States will lose all credibility as the lone superpower in the world. We have a moral obligation to fight terrorism, and Saddam might give his weapons of mass destruction to other terrorist groups. I follow the pope, and he is against the war. In military matters, I trust our president more than the pope and the president thinks we should attack. The just war tradition provides a great framework for thinking about the issue, and I agree with the American bishops that invading Iraq will do more harm than good. After giving some silent time for reflection, the pastor asked whether their decision-making process suggested that they were American Christians or Christian Americans. For you, does the cross judge the flag or vice versa? Do you pledge allegiance first to the country or to the gospel? Although a couple of people were angered by this homily and left the parish, most found that it prompted deeper reflection on a crucial issue. The pastor was grateful that the Holy Spirit gave him enough courage to overcome his fears and meet his responsibility to proclaim the social implications of the gospel. His only regret was that he did not offer an opportunity after Mass for discussion with those who were upset with the homily and felt that he took advantage of a captive audience. Prophetic preaching is an art and involves a series of prudent judgments.

Common Pastoral Situations

Wedding Homilies

Preaching at weddings presents special challenges. Couples tend to pick readings on the theme of love, especially 1 Cor 12:31–13:8, which makes it difficult to come up with fresh ideas, especially when the preacher celebrates many weddings each year. Some pastors find it hard to address couples with a meaningful word when it seems that the marriage ceremony is more of a show than a spiritual event. A preacher can often find new material and make the homily more personal by asking the couple to choose their readings prayerfully and to write out why they chose them, which images strike them, and what special meaning they carry.

Weddings are emotional occasions for many people in attendance, including those who are remembering their own wedding day. Preachers have a great opportunity to take advantage of this phenomenon by addressing portions of their homily to the married couples present. This could begin with an invitation to let their imaginations transport them back to their own wedding day and to recall how their hearts soared and their future together looked bright with promise. Now they have an opportunity to heed the Spirit who prompts them to resurrect their dream and improve their marriage in concrete ways: better communication, greater respect, renewed chemistry, a deeper shared prayer life. In a way, the newly married couple offers the gift of marriage renewal to all the married people who have been invited to share their joy. The preacher who recognizes the great opportunity to touch the hearts of the wedding guests is more likely to prepare well for the occasion and less likely to be upset by any superficial aspects of the wedding ceremony.

Funeral Homilies

Funerals also present distinctive preaching challenges. For some, the fundamental problem is to preach a homily rather than deliver a eulogy without neglecting the life of the deceased and the needs of the mourners to honor a loved one. A simple solution is to compose a regular homily focused on a specific virtue needed in the contemporary world and to use the life of the deceased as an example. For instance, a pastor knows that the deceased was very involved in feeding the hungry in the community and so he picks Matthew 25:28–35 as the Gospel. He begins the homily by discussing the rampant individualism in our culture and the common temptation to act selfishly. Then he uses the Gospel to describe an alternative approach that emphasizes helping the needy and leads to eternal life. Within that framework, he recounts concrete examples of the way the deceased man lived out the gospel ideal, grounding our hope that he now enjoys his reward. This approach may not satisfy those who oppose any form of eulogy, but it is a great way of demonstrating that Gospel ideals can make a difference in the lives of real people.

Preaching at funerals should not be glib. A wise homilist gives voice to sadness and grief. He or she knows that the ones who most love the deceased have an empty space in their hearts and their lives that cannot be filled on this earth. In tragic deaths, some mourners need a voice for their anger at God and their protest against injustice. Preachers have the difficult task of acknowledging such angry protests and placing them in a context of Christian hope.

Delivering a Homily

The standard texts on preaching offer many helpful suggestions on actually delivering sermons after completing the composition process. It is important to distinguish an oral style from a written style. Preachers who write out their sermons should try to reflect their own oral style. Some homilists deal with the problem by taping their homilies after composing a written outline. Others leave their written text behind, or take only notes to the pulpit, or leave the pulpit entirely in order to address the congregation in a more conversational fashion.

Preaching is an art, a religious event, the fruit of contemplation, an expression of our relationship to the triune God. Effective preaching is not a matter of finding the right techniques or imitating great preachers. It has to do with communicating what, in our good moments, we know to be true about the divine–human relationship definitively expressed in Jesus Christ. You will be more effective as a homilist when your style matches your personality, when you can be yourself in the act of sharing the good news with others. It does help to make eye contact with the people who are paying attention and to avoid concentrating on those who are drowsy or have developed the art of tuning out homilies. The rules for effective oral communication are important: be confident of the material; speak from the heart; match the style with the content; avoid clichés; be sure that people can hear; use appropriate gestures; use active verbs; pause at appropriate times; keep the voice up at the end of sentences; articulate clearly; and use words people can understand. Technical theological jargon is a special problem. Words that are a regular part of the preacher's vocabulary are often foreign to parishioners—even common words like God, grace, revelation, salvation, and redemption need clarification or alternative phrasing. We could express those great realities in other ways: for example, the gracious One (God) shares the divine life with us (grace) that lights our path (revelation), heals our wounds (salvation), and brings fulfillment to the deepest longings of our heart (redemption). Homilies with fresh language and new images to express traditional teachings have a better chance of touching the minds and hearts of the assembly.

Sometimes a preacher can find more creative ways of delivering the message: using visual props, including film clips, eliciting responses from the congregation. It is relatively easy to invite a brief one-to-one conversation on a particular point in the homily. Dialogue homilies that involve the whole congregation are more difficult. They seem to work best in smaller groups and on special occasions, such as Thanksgiving. In initiating the dialogue, the preacher should ask people to share some experience that exemplifies the focus, rather than to offer an opinion on a doctrinal point or express a personal feeling on a controversial issue. This roots the dialogue in real life and highlights the common character of the human adventure.

Feedback

Constructive feedback is a useful instrument for improving preaching. Preachers get initial feedback from the faces of those listening to the homily: interested, bored, quizzical, upset. These spontaneous reactions are generally more reliable than the positive comments at the end of the service, which are often simply polite expressions of appreciation and gratitude. We know if someone was really touched by a homily if weeks later they are still talking about it and putting the message into practice.

A homilist can take a more active role in seeking feedback: handing out evaluation sheets to the whole congregation on a given week; asking a faith-sharing group for honest reaction; eliciting comments from trusted friends; listening to a tape of a homily with a person skilled in communications. Preachers who gather in small groups to watch and critique videotapes of one another's homilies report that they learn ways to improve not only from the honest criticism but also from the practices of their colleagues. Feedback is important to homilists who recognize the significance of the preaching ministry and are open to constructive criticism.

KEVIN ANDERSON RESPONSE

I think this is the chapter in which Jim's quality of being attuned to listeners' human concerns really breaks through. His many questions highlighting listener concerns can serve as helpful guides to preachers who wonder whether they are hitting close to the heart of human experience when they speak in the pulpit.

In this chapter Jim got down to the "nitty gritty." How do you come up with ideas to fill out the homily so that it is not a vague presentation that fails to grab listeners' attention and imagination? Where do creative ideas for stories, metaphors, and illustrations come from? Jim suggests that the elements of a good homily do not appear "special delivery" from the Holy Spirit to preachers who are not intentional about their preparation to preach. Good preaching has something to do with tuning in.

Intentional Preparation

Jim has referred to distant preparation (personal development and knowing the congregation) and proximate preparation (the week of the homily). I want to introduce the term *intentional* preparation. Intentional simply means *on purpose*, as opposed to haphazard or by a stroke of luck. It seems to me that Jim's emphasis on early determination of a focus allows a preacher's entire week to inform the homily. If the preacher makes a regular practice of determining a focus early, he or she sets some intentional energy into motion that invites material for the homily throughout the week. By centering the mind and spirit on the readings early in the week, the preacher intentionally puts her- or himself on alert for material that will bring the homily to life.

This is a creative process. When a birdwatcher has her binoculars out and is actively scanning for birds, the species count rises. When a poet tunes in to a theme (such as grief), ordinary events begin to present themselves as metaphors for grief. For instance, witnessing a dog drag a baby raccoon from the woods and kill it (as I did recently) could be just a brief incident to observe and forget. But if one's spirit is on alert for metaphors for suffering and loss, the incident becomes an invitation to reflect on the suddenness with which difficulty can appear in this incarnated existence and to ponder why bad things happen with no warning.

On the Alert

Jim's use of the phrase "on the alert"—encouraging preachers to stay awake for possibilities for the homily during the week—seems important to me. I knew one preacher who regularly talked about not being prepared to preach. He said he relied on the Holy Spirit to move him at the moment of the homily. I wouldn't accept such thinking from a surgeon ("I didn't review your record—I'm just counting on my skill to carry the day during the surgery"). I think the spiritually hungry people in the pews need the kind of deliberate preparation that Jim is advocating.

There's a saying among poets that the muse shows up to the poet who shows up. This means that waiting around for inspiration to move you to write is not as effective as actually sitting down with pen in hand and tuning in to what presents itself. I think this is similar to what Jim is encouraging for preachers. Center your spirit early in the week on a focus—"show up" to the preparation process—and inspiration will begin showing up in the remainder of the week in the form of metaphors, interesting stories, turns of phrase, and so on. When we get our attention focused, we invite what we need to make itself apparent.

Here's a story to illustrate the point. Several years ago, a few months after my father died, I was still feeling quite heavy with the loss. One Saturday I decided to put together a kit for a bluebird box that I'd had for some time. As I assembled it, I felt that I was wasting my time, because I'd never seen a bluebird on our property in the eight years we'd been there. The day after I nailed the box to a fencepost just forty feet from our home, two bluebirds showed up. It was quickly apparent to me that the birds had been there all along. Until I built the box, I had not been attentive for them, had not become intentional about seeing them, so I thought they were not there. When we focus our attention, good things start coming our way. Setting a focus for the homily is like building your box early in the week. Then you can keep tuned in for what shows up.

I want to emphasize how important this process seems to me. We live in a hyperactive culture that has, in the words of Hugh Hewitt in *Searching for God in America* (Dallas: Word, 1996), "eviscerated the opportunity for reflection." The average person sitting in front of a preacher on Sunday is not having a great deal of success carving out quiet prayer time. In fact, she or he may have lost a sense that it is important to do so, may be under the illusion that there is no time, and may be counting on you to make up in fifteen minutes on Sunday for her or his lack of daily contemplation. A preacher who himself lives entirely in the frenetic pace of the culture is less likely to deliver a homily that hits home than one who is intentional about creating time to contemplate the Scripture and determine focus and function well in advance of the service.

Use of Personal Stories

Jim suggests that personal stories can be effective but come with the risk that they will annoy listeners or distract from the focus. To me, the key issue is whether the homilist uses a personal story as only one small part of elucidating the human concern that is addressed in the focus. A brief personal story followed by several other composite stories conveys to listeners, "I know this concern personally and I have heard about the same concern from many others." When used appropriately, self-disclosure can facilitate the crucial variable "knows what is in my heart." Listeners are not afraid of or put off by the preacher's humanness. They know the difference, however, between a preacher who discloses his or her own experience to enlighten others and one who is taking too much time on oneself. I agree with Jim that trivial revelations about such things as vacations are less effective than personal stories that speak directly to the focus for the week.

Whether or not you liked the self-disclosure in my bluebird story several paragraphs back may be an indicator of which side you lean to (more or less use of personal material).

Sequence

In presenting the focus, the homilist has two choices: begin with the human concern, or begin with Scripture. I like Jim's

guideline of mixing it up. I also concur that too much time elucidating Scripture without tying it to a here-and-now human concern risks losing the listener to all of the other chatter in her or
his mind. A preacher should treat the listener's attention as the
sine qua non of the homily. Without it you have nothing; with it
you can change lives.

Our preaching data speak to the question of sequence. We
asked listeners whether their preachers first elucidated the
Scriptures or first presented the human concern. Listeners were
slightly more likely to rate a preacher as effective if she or he
started with the Scriptures. But both approaches were positively
related to preacher effectiveness ratings. More research would be
needed to determine if one approach or the other is generally
more effective. This may not be a simple matter, as one style
could work better for some congregations, the other for different
congregations.

Content and Process

Jim's concluding thoughts on how the homily should be
delivered are helpful. Yet they are the only pages in this book that
deal with the "how" of delivery (versus the "what"—the content
of the homily). Focus and function deal mostly with content—
what you'll say in your homily. *How* you deliver the homily—with
enthusiasm, with good nonverbals (eye contact, gestures, voice
tone, volume, and speed)—influences how the message is
received. The data presented in the appendix make it clear, however, that these variables of process ("how") are less correlated to
preacher effectiveness ratings than the content variables. It
appears from our data that good content can somewhat compen-
sate for ineffective nonverbals, but good nonverbals cannot make
up for inadequate, unfocused, or shallow content.

JAMES BACIK RESPONSE

Kevin's concluding comments on the relationship between
content (the "what") and the delivery (the "how") of a homily
invites further reflection. Our survey material does support the

emphasis on content found throughout this book. Perhaps we should give more attention, however, to the organic connection between the specific content and the style of delivery. For example, an Easter homily on the joy of the resurrection in a world shaken by violence should soar. The delivery should be enthusiastic and the language should touch the soul and lift the spirit. A sermon on improving family life can be delivered with a more down-to-earth didactic style.

In a homily on the story of the Prodigal Son (Luke 15:11–32), I decided to focus on the encounter between the father and the older son. My key insight was that the father continued to think of the prodigal as his son even though he had taken his inheritance and distanced himself from the family. The older son, on the other hand, wanted to disown his brother and exclude him from the family. I was confident that this point could be developed into an effective response to our common temptation to refuse forgiveness to those who have hurt us and to exclude them from our lives. The father avoided this temptation by keeping alive the memory of his son and refusing to treat him as a hired hand. He understood that relationships are more important than misconduct, failures, and the violation of social customs. This insight grounds his ability to forgive his son and his spontaneous desire to celebrate his return.

While struggling to work out a proper sequence for this material, I decided to cast the whole homily as an imagined response of the father to his son's refusal to go into the party, and to deliver it sitting down. I actually wrote out the father's monologue and read most of it. After inviting the congregation to listen in and stay alert for a personal message, I began: "My son I know you are hurt. Everything you say is true. You have been a wonderful son, always obedient and never a troublemaker. I probably have taken you for granted and I am sorry for that." The father then goes on to speak to his son in familiar terms that contain important advice: try to feel good about your loyal service; relationships are more important than misdeeds; memory is crucial in preserving relationships; forgiveness is the only way to rise above hurts; hanging on to anger is self-destructive and leads to demonizing the other. Throughout the monologue, the father speaks from his heart: "When your brother left I, too, was hurt, but he always remained my son. I remembered my joy when he was born and my delight in watching you two play together." I concluded the homily with the father asking his son (and by inference the congregation) to take time to pray over his decision about the party. He added: "You will always be my son no matter what you decide, but I hope we can go to the party together and both embrace the one who was dead and is now alive—my son and your brother."

The positive feedback on this homily suggested that the method of delivery (sitting and reading a monologue) had reinforced the content. One woman told me she never saw so many teary-eyed men at Mass—something I did not notice, since I had no eye contact with the assembly. More significantly, weeks later, individuals were still telling me they remembered the point of the homily and were reaching out to embrace someone who had hurt them. The example suggests the importance of delivering the homily in a style that reflects the content. Kevin is right—a good delivery cannot make up for shallow content, but it can enhance solid material.

Kevin suggested to me privately that I put a schematic summary of the main points of the book in the introduction. I bought the notion of listing practical ideas found in each chapter, but thought it would fit better at the end of the book after we had established a framework for appreciating the advice.

1. Recognize the importance of preaching and put our best efforts into homily preparation. Pray for guidance. Start preparing early in the week. Stay alert for good material.

2. Attend to our own personal growth, especially intellectually and spiritually, as a critical component of preaching more effectively.

3. Listen well to our parishioners in order to understand better their joys and challenges and to respond to their needs.

4. Engage the Scripture readings with a critical mind and a prayerful, open heart. Consult good commentaries.

5. Develop a focus point for each homily, one that includes an existential concern and a biblical insight. Avoid thematic approaches that are disconnected from real life.

6. Determine the function of the homily, the personal or social transformation desired.

7. Illustrate both elements of the focus with relevant stories, good examples, and realistic descriptions.

8. Compose introductions that gain attention and lead into the dynamic of the focus point and conclusions that reinforce the function.

9. Use a style of delivery that fits our personality and the content of the homily.

10. Learn from honest feedback how to improve our preaching.

I want to thank Kevin Anderson for all his insightful comments, which reflect his experience as an attentive hearer of the Word and a very effective psychotherapist. The appendix that follows contains more of his suggestions as well as the statistical material gathered in preparation for this book.

Preacher Effectiveness Data from Four Samples of Listeners

This appendix focuses on a survey completed by over 2,000 listeners rating 136 different preachers. In the data presented below, listeners tell us through their survey ratings how they evaluate preaching.

The Survey

Design of the Survey

The survey used to collect data from the four samples of listeners described later (national, Catholic priest, Catholic deacon, and workshop samples) was designed by the two authors. The content of the items was in part determined by the results of a national survey of preacher training conducted by the authors. In that survey, forty-two experts in training preachers at seminaries around the United States gave opinions about effective and ineffective preaching. In addition to yielding other interesting findings beyond the scope of this book, the preacher training survey led to seven items for the listener survey that forms the core of the data presented in this appendix. The theoretical questions and interests of the authors led to the creation of the other twenty-nine items.

We decided to phrase some questions in a positive manner (for example, "This preacher is a very likable person") and some in a negative manner (for example, "This preacher speaks too much in a monotone voice"). This decision was made to prevent respondents from quickly filling out the survey with all positive or all negative ratings without carefully reading each survey item. When data analyses were completed, negative questions were not as useful as the positive questions in predicting ratings of preacher effectiveness in these four samples. It may be that negative questions are most appropriate for studies of *ineffective* preaching.

Key Language Used in the Survey

The word *preacher* was used throughout the survey to describe the person who delivers the sermon or homily. This was seen as the most generic term for a survey that was used across multiple Christian denominations in the national sample. The word *sermon* was used to describe the preaching event in the survey. This term is more familiar today to Protestants, but it was felt that Catholics (who usually refer to "homilies") would understand the term *sermon*.

Predictor Variables

The survey contained thirty-six "predictor variables" that were individual survey items designed to help us study a particular aspect of preaching. (These thirty-six survey items are listed in table 7 on p. 162, which gives the composite rankings of all the predictors we studied.) The example below illustrates why these survey items are called "predictors":

PREDICTOR VARIABLE   SAMPLE RATING VARIABLE

This preacher is a very   This preacher gives effective
likable person.   sermons.

The predictor variable measured the respondents' opinions about preachers and various aspects of the approaches they use in their preaching. The rating variables (see section below) more directly measured the respondents' opinions about the effectiveness of the preachers' sermons.

Each predictor variable (survey item) was answered using the following six-point scale:

1	2	3	4	5	6
Strongly Disagree	Disagree	Slightly Disagree	Slightly Agree	Agree	Strongly Agree

Note that a "neutral" point was not included in the scale, so that respondents had at least to indicate slight agreement or disagreement with each statement.

Rating Variables

Five survey items were used to assess the respondents' rating of the preacher's effectiveness. These items were:

1. This preacher gives effective sermons.
2. This preacher's sermons come to mind throughout the week following the service.
3. This preacher gives sermons that I like.
4. This preacher's sermons help me reflect on the meaning and purpose of life.
5. This preacher's sermons help me take specific actions to lead a better life.

Respondents used the same six-point scale used for the predictor variables to respond to the rating variables.

Data analysis showed that answers to the five rating variables were highly correlated and appeared to reflect an underlying global assessment of preacher effectiveness. Therefore, these five variables were summed together to create an overall rating variable that served as a global rating of the preacher's perceived effectiveness.

The Four Samples of Listeners

National Sample (1994)

The national sample consisted of sixty-two people from fifteen cities in the United States who responded to the survey that was mailed to their homes. Six hundred surveys were mailed to residents picked randomly from the telephone directories of fifteen cities in the United States. The response rate was 10.3 percent. While this response rate is not low for a mailed survey, the sample size is still quite small. See table 1 for specific sample characteristics. Of the fifty-nine preachers whose gender was specified, fifty-five were men and four were women. Sixty-one of the sixty-two respondents stated that their ratings were based on a specific preacher whom they had seen. One respondent rated her experience of preachers in general.

Catholic Priests Sample (1994)

The Catholic priests sample consisted of 1,115 Catholics who answered the survey to rate thirty-four priests, using the survey after hearing the priests preach at Sunday Mass in the Catholic Diocese of Toledo, Ohio, during the fall of 1994. Surveys were handed out at the end of Mass and completed immediately or returned later to the parish. See table 1 for specific sample characteristics.

Catholic Deacons Sample (1994)

The Catholic deacons sample consisted of 813 Catholics who used the survey to rate thirty-five deacons after hearing them preach at Mass in the fall of 1994. Surveys were handed out at the end of Mass and completed immediately or returned later to the parish. See table 1 for specific sample characteristics.

Workshop Sample (2002)

In 2002, participants at a preaching workshop taught by both authors were invited to send in survey data from their congregations for data analysis. Five preachers (four Catholic priests and one male Protestant pastor) sent in a total of 180 surveys. The survey used for this sample was an abbreviated form of the one used in the other three samples. It included sixteen of the thirty-six original items, those deemed to be of most interest for further research.

Table 1: Demographics for the National, Priests, and Deacons Samples of Listeners

Variable	National Sample	Catholic Priests Sample	Catholic Deacons Sample
Total number of respondents	62	1,115	813
Number of preachers rated	62	34	35
Gender of respondents	28 men 34 women 0 unspecified	397 men 697 women 21 unspecified	270 men 476 women 67 unspecified
Race of respondents	57 Caucasian 3 African Am. 0 Hispanic 0 Asian 2 Other	1,027 Caucasian 14 African Am. 10 Hispanic 8 Asian 56 Other	696 Caucasian 12 African Am. 13 Hispanic 11 Asian 81 Other
Marital status of respondents	8 Never married 39 Married 8 Remarried 5 Divorced 2 Widowed	106 Never married 772 Married 59 Remarried 46 Divorced 92 Widowed 40 Unspecified	72 Never married 520 Married 33 Remarried 32 Divorced 80 Widowed 76 Unspecified
Average number of children	1.8	4.3	4.7
Average age of respondents	44.0	52.5	54.6
Average household income	$44,000/yr.	$44,000/yr.	$39,000/yr.
Average years of education	15.7	14.9	13.8
Average times/yr. attending religious services	51.6	88.9	114.6
Preacher's gender	55 men 4 women 3 unspecified	34 men	35 men
Preacher's average age (as perceived by listener)	50.0	50.8	53.0

The total of 180 surveys on five preachers is an admittedly small sample, but it was collected as an attempt to replicate the 1994 findings. Small samples lead to what statisticians call "low statistical power" (difficulty detecting things in the data), but this fourth sample provided results remarkably similar to those found several years earlier. When samples with low statistical power still reveal an effect, it appears that the effect is a strong one (easily detectable even in small samples).

Note: The first three samples (national, priests, deacons) are referred to collectively in the appendix as the "1994 samples" (referring to the year they were collected).

Note: Demographics were not collected for participants in the "Workshop" sample gathered in 2002.

Summary of Sample Characteristics

All three samples in which demographics were collected had more women than men (55 percent in the national sample, 64 percent in both the priests and deacons samples), were predominantly Caucasian, and included almost exclusively male preachers (only 4 of 131 preachers rated were specified as female). The average respondent in all three samples had some college and a middle-class income (approximately $40,000 to $45,000 per year). The average preacher rated was perceived to be approximately 50 to 53 years old.

The four samples were not randomly obtained and do not describe a scientific cross-section of the United States population. Therefore, the potential for generalizing the results of this study is tentative until further research on larger and more representative samples is obtained.

Results of Data Analysis

Rating Variables Summed to Give Overall Rating

Table 2 (on page 155) summarizes respondents' answers to the five variables used to gauge their ratings of preacher effectiveness. These averages refer to the six-point scale (in which 4 = slightly agree; 5 = agree; 6 = strongly agree).

Statistical analysis indicated that answers to these five individual survey items were highly correlated. Therefore, responses on these five items were totaled to give an overall rating score. This overall rating score was used as the primary measure of preacher effectiveness in the remaining statistical analyses.

The average ratings of preachers on these five items across the samples was in the "slightly agree" to "agree" range, except for the "workshop" sample. The results from these samples do not indicate strong dissatisfaction with preaching, nor do they reflect a resounding approval of preaching. Because each person who completed a survey in all three samples did so completely voluntarily, it is possible that a "selection bias" affected these results. This would be the case, for instance, if persons more satisfied with preaching were systematically more likely to complete a survey than those with more negative opinions. Similarly, the priests and deacons who chose to collect data from their listeners did so on a voluntary basis. It is possible that more confident or skilled preachers chose to include themselves in this study, and therefore biased the overall ratings of preachers in the positive direction. As an initial study of this kind, this study was not capable of determining how much selection bias may have affected these results. Further research will need to address such concerns.

Table 2: Average Ratings of Preachers on Five Individual Rating Items across National, Priests, Deacons, and Workshop Samples

Rating Item	Avg. Rating, National Sample	Avg. Rating, Priests Sample	Avg. Rating, Deacons Sample	Avg. Rating, Workshop Sample
This preacher gives effective sermons.	4.77	4.99	4.95	(not measured)
This preacher's sermons come to mind throughout the week following the service.	3.92	4.17	4.04	(not measured)
This preacher gives sermons that I like.	4.56	4.80	4.82	(not measured)
This preacher's sermons help me reflect on the meaning and purpose of life.	4.61	4.83	4.77	(not measured)
This preacher's sermons help me take specific actions to lead a better life.	4.26	4.64	4.57	(not measured)

It is also interesting to note that the two rating items that asked respondents about how the sermons affected them *after* the sermon (how much the sermon comes to mind the following week, how much the sermon leads to specific actions to lead a better life) were rated lower than the items asking for the effectiveness, likability, or ability to help the listener reflect on the meaning and purpose of life. It appears that sermons are perceived more positively for what they offer *during the service* than for their lasting impact. In counseling, this issue is referred to as the "transfer of training" issue: Do people in counseling transfer their learning in counseling to their day-to-day lives? The results of this study on preaching suggest "transfer of training" may be an interesting area for further preaching research.

Single Survey Item Predictors of Ratings of Preacher Effectiveness

There are two major ways to analyze the thirty-six predictor variables (survey items):

1. Consider each predictor variable individually. How much does this one predictor explain about how listeners rated preachers in each of the four samples?
2. Consider the ability of the predictor questions in subgroups to explain the variability in how preachers were rated. Which combination of predictors best accounts for the variability in how preachers were rated?

This section will discuss the individual predictor variables in each of the four samples (national, priests, deacons, workshop) that were most highly correlated with the overall rating of preacher effectiveness. A later section (Analyses of Several Predictors Considered Together, p. 171) will consider the ability of certain subgroups of predictors to explain variance in overall preacher ratings.

The top predictor questions in the national, priests, deacons, and workshop samples are presented in tables 3 to 6. The numbers in the right-hand columns of these tables indicate the percent of the variation in ratings of preachers in each sample that can be explained using each predictor variable alone. Statisticians call this the R-squared, but for our purposes, the higher the number, the more predictive that survey item is of listeners' ratings of preacher effectiveness in that sample.

When we speak of "variation" or "variability" in ratings of preachers, we are referring to the fact that each person who completed a survey on a particular preacher rated that preacher in a unique fashion. That is, ratings of the *same* preacher vary from rater to rater. This variability is interesting to researchers when it is systematic or predictable. In the national sample, for example, 79 percent of the variability in the overall rating of the preacher's effectiveness could be predicted by knowing how the respondent answered the question "This preacher's sermons make me feel like he or she knows what is in my heart." On average, only 21 percent of the variability in the preacher rating is left unexplained in that sample when we know the respondent's answer to the "knows what is in my heart" predictor.

Remember, some survey items were phrased positively and some were phrased negatively. Both positive and negative items can explain systematic variability in a set of data. However, the "direction" of their relationship to the rating variable is opposite. In tables 3 to 6, a "+" sign next to the percentage figure in the right-hand column means that the predictor variable is positively related to the rating variable. That is, the higher a person scores the preacher on this predictor variable, the higher the score on the preacher effectiveness variable is likely to be.

Were a "-" (minus sign) to appear, this would mean that the higher a preacher was scored on the predictor, the lower the preacher was scored on the rating variable. For instance, if a respondent gave a preacher a high score (strongly agree) on the predictor "speaks too much in a monotone voice," the respondent was more likely to give the preacher a relatively low rating on overall effectiveness. However, none of the top individual predictor variables in the four samples had a negative (-) relationship to the overall rating variable.

Table 3: The Top Individual Predictors of Preacher Ratings in the National Sample (N = 62 listeners who rated 62 preachers)

Percent Variation in Preacher Ratings
Explained by This Predictor Alone

This preacher's sermons make me feel like he or she knows what is in my heart.	79 (+)
The preacher's style of delivering the sermon helps keep my attention.	76 (+)
This preacher's sermons are relevant to my daily life.	69 (+)
This preacher's sermons usually have a clear central message.	56 (+)
This preacher uses natural and effective gestures while preaching.	55 (+)
This preacher's sermons are well-prepared.	50 (+)
This preacher helps me get a new or deeper appreciation of the Scripture readings.	50 (+)
This preacher makes creative use of stories and examples to enhance the sermon.	49 (+)
This preacher knows the real struggles of life.	48 (+)
This preacher uses humor effectively in sermons.	45 (+)

Table 4: The Top Individual Predictors of Preacher Ratings in the Catholic Priests Sample (N = 1,115 listeners who rated 34 priests)

Percent Variation in Preacher Ratings
Explained by This Predictor Alone

This preacher's style of delivering the sermon helps keep my attention.	67 (+)
This preacher's sermons make me feel like he or she knows what is in my heart.	66 (+)
This preacher's sermons are relevant to my daily life.	59 (+)
This preacher makes creative use of stories or examples to enhance the sermon.	56 (+)
This preacher uses humor effectively in sermons.	55 (+)
This preacher's sermons usually have a clear central message.	55 (+)
This preacher helps me get a new or deeper appreciation of the Scripture reading(s).	55 (+)
This preacher is a very likable person.	50 (+)
This preacher knows the real struggles of life.	48 (+)
This preacher usually presents ideas in the sermon very similar to my own.	44 (+)

Table 5: The Top Individual Predictors of Preacher Ratings in the Catholic Deacons Sample (N = 813 listeners who rated 35 deacons)

Percent Variation in Preacher Ratings
Explained by This Predictor Alone

This preacher helps me get a new or deeper appreciation of the Scripture reading(s).	52 (+)
This preacher's style of delivering the sermon helps keep my attention.	50 (+)
This preacher's sermons usually have a clear central message.	46 (+)
This preacher makes creative use of stories or examples to enhance the sermon.	45 (+)
This preacher uses humor effectively in sermons.	41 (+)
This preacher's sermons make me feel like he or she knows what is in my heart.	38 (+)
This preacher usually presents ideas in the sermon very similar to my own.	35 (+)
This preacher's sermons are relevant to my daily life.	30 (+)
This preacher is a well-trained expert in Scripture.	27 (+)
This preacher is a very likable person.	24 (+)
This preacher has good eye contact with the congregation during the sermon.	24 (+)

Table 6: The Top Individual Predictors of Preacher Ratings in the Workshop Sample (N = 180 listeners who rated 5 preachers)

Percent Variation in Preacher Ratings
Explained by This Predictor Alone

This preacher's sermons make me feel like he or she knows what is in my heart.	41 (+)
This preacher's sermons usually have a clear central message.	41 (+)
This preacher usually presents ideas in the sermon very similar to my own.	40 (+)
This preacher's style of delivering the sermon helps keep my attention.	39 (+)
This preacher helps me get a new or deeper appreciation of the scripture readings.	37 (+)
This preacher's sermons are relevant to my daily life.	29 (+)

Note: Percent variance predicted is the smallest in this sample because it has the smallest sample size (5 preachers rated by 180 listeners). The national sample had only 62 listeners, but they rated 62 different preachers, which gives more statistical power.

Composite Rankings of Individual Predictors

Each predictor item (e.g., "This preacher is a very likable person") was assigned a rank within each 1994 sample (national, priest, deacon). (The workshop sample was excluded from this analysis because it collected data on only 16 of the 36 predictors.) The more predictive the item was of the summed RATING variable, the higher the rank it received. Then the rankings for each item were averaged across the three 1994 samples to arrive at a composite ranking for each item. The results are presented in table 7.

Table 7: Composite Rankings of All 36 Predictors of Preacher Ratings across the National, Priests, and Deacons Samples

Survey Item (Survey Question Number Indicated in Parentheses)	Composite Rank	National, Priest, Deacon Sample Ranks	Average Percent of Rating Predicted Across Three Samples
This preacher's style of delivering the sermon helps keep my attention. (Q24)	1	2, 1, 2	64% +
This preacher's sermons make me feel like he or she knows what is in my heart. (Q39)	2	1, 1, 6	60% +
This preacher helps me get a new or deeper appreciation of the Scripture readings. (Q21)	3	6, 5, 1	53% +
This preacher's sermons usually have a clear central message. (Q20)	4	4, 5, 3	52% +
This preacher's sermons are relevant to my daily life. (Q32)	5	3, 3, 8	51% +
This preacher makes creative use of stories and examples to enhance the sermon. (Q52)	6	8, 4, 4	50% +

Survey Item (Survey Question Number Indicated in Parentheses)	Composite Rank	National, Priest, Deacon Sample Ranks	Average Percent of Rating Predicted Across Three Samples
This preacher uses humor effectively in sermons. (Q41)	7	10, 5, 5	47% +
This preacher usually presents ideas in the sermon very similar to my own. (Q51)	8	15, 10, 7	38% +
This preacher is a very likable person. (Q18)	9	14, 8, 10	36% +
This preacher knows the real struggles of life. (Q40)	10	9, 9, 19	35% +
This preacher uses natural and effective gestures while preaching. (Q27)	11	5, 15, 15	32% +
This preacher has good eye contact with the congregation during the sermon. (Q25)	12	12, 13, 10	31% +
This preacher's sermons are well-prepared. (Q23)	13	6, 18, 15	30% +
This preacher's experience of daily life is similar to mine. (Q47)	14	11, 17, 17	28% +
This preacher appears to have a poor understanding of the needs of the congregation. (Q31)	15	16, 11, 19	26% -
This preacher seems to have a strong faith and prayer life. (Q17)	16	15, 13, 18	26% +
This preacher lacks enthusiasm while giving the sermon. (Q30)	17	21, 15, 13	25% -
This preacher shares significant personal experiences in sermons. (Q42)	18	20, 11, 19	25% +
This preacher usually explains the scripture readings first and then applies them to real life. (Q35)	19	24, 21, 12	22% +

Survey Item (Survey Question Number Indicated in Parentheses)	Composite Rank	National, Priest, Deacon Sample Ranks	Average Percent of Rating Predicted Across Three Samples
This preacher makes use of valuable insights from other sources such as poetry, literature, psychology, or philosophy. (Q44)	19	24, 19, 13	22% +
This preacher's sermons are poorly organized. (Q22)	21	21, 25, 23	19% -
This preacher lacks personal integrity. (Q38)	22	13, 20, 32	18% -
This preacher speaks too much in a monotone voice. (Q29)	23	18, 23, 22	17% -
This preacher speaks loudly and clearly enough to be heard and understood. (Q28)	24	19, 27, 27	16% +
This preacher usually describes a human concern first and then uses the Scripture readings to help listeners understand and deal with them better. (Q25)	25	25, 24, 25	15% +
This preacher is a well-trained expert in Scripture. (Q33)	26	27, 30, 9	15% +
This preacher mostly talks in sermons about things that happened a long time ago. (Q37)	27	23, 21, 35	13% -
This preacher usually presents ideas in the sermons that are very different from my own. (Q49)	28	27, 26, 26	12% -
This preacher bases his/her preaching on the Scripture passages read at the service. (Q19)	29	31, 28, 24	11% +
This preacher has a basically negative attitude about our culture. (Q43)	30	30, 29, 32	8% -

Survey Item (Survey Question Number Indicated in Parentheses)	Composite Rank	National, Priest, Deacon Sample Ranks	Average Percent of Rating Predicted Across Three Samples
This preacher is open to and tolerant of other religions. (Q45)	31	29, 31, 31	7% +
This preacher usually reads all or most of the sermon. (Q26)	32	31, 34, 27	6% -
This preacher seldom discusses social concerns of peace and justice. (Q46)	33	35, 32, 29	4% -
This preacher discusses in sermons the things that sometimes make living a good life difficult. (Q48)	34	33, 33, 36	3% +
This preacher usually uses literal interpretations of the Scripture readings. (Q34)	35	36, 35, 29	3% +
This preacher usually presents ideas in the sermon that are somewhat different from and somewhat similar to my own. (Q50)	36	34, 35, 34	2% +

Discussion of Composite Rankings

The ten individual predictors most related to overall rating of preacher effectiveness, as determined by composite ranks across all three 1994 samples of listeners, are discussed below. These are referred to as the "top ten" predictors throughout the main text of the book.

Keeps my attention. This predictor emerged as the most powerful in the survey when used alone. It was ranked second in the national sample, first in the priests sample, and second in the deacons sample. Nearly two-thirds (64 percent, averaged across the three samples) of the variability in how people in these samples rated preachers could be predicted by their evaluation of how well the preacher held their attention.

This finding is consistent with communication theory. If the listener's attention is not maintained, the message does not register and the effectiveness of the communication is seriously compromised.

Knows what is in my heart. Anecdotal evidence suggests that people are moved by sermons that make the listener feel like the preacher was "speaking directly to me." The data from the three 1994 samples supports this. In the national sample, nearly 80 percent of the variability in how preachers were rated could be predicted with this one item. The item was ranked first and second in the national and priests sample respectively, but only sixth in the deacons sample. Perhaps Catholic listeners assume that deacons are aware of what is in their hearts because their daily lives are more similar to the lives of those in the congregation. This predictor may have more explanatory power for priests than deacons because priests are perceived as more dissimilar to listeners than are deacons. (On the item "This preacher's experience of daily life is similar to mine," priests' average rating was 3.29 [on scale of 1–6, 1 = strongly disagree, 6 = strongly agree], deacons' average rating was 4.07.)

Helps me get a new or deeper appreciation of Scripture. While this item was ranked third overall, accounting for 53 percent of the variability in preacher ratings across the three 1994 samples, it was particularly predictive for deacons (ranked number one in the deacons sample). This may be because deacons tend to be weaker in Scripture training than priests. Deacons who are seen as well versed in Scripture are rated more highly as preachers than their peers who are seen as less knowledgeable about Scripture.

Clear central message. Many complaints about preaching are related to rambling, lack of focus, "going off on tangents." The data from the 1994 samples corroborates the importance of a clear central message in the sermon. When used alone as a predictor, this variable predicted on average 52 percent of the variability in ratings of preachers.

Relevant to my daily life. Data from these samples supports the idea that sermons should not focus "back there" (on Bible history) or "up there" (in theological discussion), but rather on matters of relevance to the daily lives of listeners. This predictor was ranked third in the national and priests sample, but only eighth in the deacons sample. It is not clear why this variable was able to explain nearly twice as much variability in ratings of priests (59 percent) as compared to deacons (30 percent). This finding may indicate that priests have a greater gap to bridge to be perceived as relevant, because their experience of daily life is perceived as being less similar to the congregation's than that of deacons. If there is greater variability from priest to priest than from deacon to deacon on ability to preach with relevance to listeners' lives, the relevance predictor would be more crucial for explaining ratings of preacher effectiveness for priests than for deacons.

Creative use of stories and examples. In the national sample, this predictor was ranked eighth in predictive power. In both the Catholic samples, it was ranked fourth. The importance of stories and examples fits well with research on human memory. Stories may create images, feelings, and insights that serve to create a "deep processing" of the central message of the sermon. It is well documented in memory research that messages processed in such a way (connecting the message to images, feelings, and stories) are remembered longer than those that are delivered in words only.

Effective use of humor. This variable was also rated higher in the two Catholic samples (fifth in both the priests and deacons samples) than in the national sample (tenth). Humor used effectively can help maintain attention. Humor may also be a common human language that helps the listener perceive the preacher as one who understands the human condition. More research is necessary to determine how listeners respond to both effective and ineffective attempts at humor in preaching.

Similarity of ideas. Social psychological research predicts that people are most receptive to messages that are similar to what they already believe. For instance, when left in a waiting room, smokers were found to be more likely to read material about the benefits of smoking than nonsmokers. The findings of the 1994 samples support this theory. Consider the three survey items and their overall rank according to their ability to predict how a preacher is rated (table 8):

Table 8: Composite Rankings of Strong, Weak, and Moderate Preacher/Listener Similarity Predictors of Preacher Ratings

	Composite Rank	Avg. % of Rating Predicted Across 1994 Samples
This preacher usually presents ideas in the sermon very similar to my own.	8 +	38%
This preacher usually presents ideas very different from my own.	28 -	12%
This preacher usually presents ideas in the sermon that are somewhat different from and somewhat similar to my own.	36 +	2%

These results mean, for instance, that the predictor item "This preacher usually presents ideas in the sermon very different from my own" was ranked twenty-eighth out of thirty-six predictors and had a negative relationship to preacher ratings. That is, the higher the agreement with this item, the lower the preacher rating.

Note that the "somewhat different/somewhat similar" predictor item was the least predictive item in the entire survey. A number of respondents remarked that this item was worded in a confusing manner. Confusing items lose predictive ability because respondents answer them in erratic rather than predictable ways. Further research should investigate moderate preacher/listener similarity using a more simply worded item.

The findings in table 8 suggest that challenging a congregation with ideas that are very different from the ideas most of the listeners already hold is difficult territory for a preacher. Further research is necessary to determine which factors allow preachers to address controversial topics effectively without being tuned out by listeners.

This preacher is a very likable person. The listener's global assessment of the preacher as a person—presumably formed in part from experiences beyond the preaching context—has an impact on how the preacher is evaluated. A well-liked preacher may be more likely to command attention and may be more capable of challenging listeners with difficult messages. A listener is not likely to conclude that a preacher "knows what is in my heart" if the listener does not like the preacher. The effectiveness of what a preacher does in the pulpit appears to be affected by the quality of his or her relationships with the people in the congregation.

Knows the real struggles of life. The wording of this item appears similar to "knows what is in my heart." While this survey item was ranked ninth for the national and priests samples, it was only nineteenth for the deacons sample. Again, Catholic listeners may take for granted that deacons know the struggles of life because their daily experience of life is perceived as similar to the experience of those in the congregation.

Discussion of Nonverbal Predictors

Many communication experts contend that the majority of the meaning of a communication is carried in the nonverbal channels. "Nonverbals" include all aspects of communication that are separate from the words or verbal content of the communication. These include eye contact, gestures, tone and loudness of voice, and enthusiasm. The survey items in table 9 (on the next page) were related specifically to nonverbals.

Table 9: Composite Rankings of Nonverbal Predictors of Preacher Ratings

	Composite Rank	Avg. % of Rating Predicted Across Three Samples
This preacher uses natural and effective gestures while preaching.	11	32% +
This preacher has good eye contact with the congregation during the sermon.	12	31% +
This preacher lacks enthusiasm while giving the sermon.	17	25% -
This preacher speaks too much in a monotone voice.	23	17% -
This preacher speaks loudly and clearly enough to be heard and understood.	24	16% +
This preacher usually reads all or most of the sermon.	32	6% -

While the nonverbals as a group are not ranked as highly as a number of other predictors, they emerge from the data as important factors in how preachers are rated. Based on these data, for instance, nearly one third (32 percent) of a listener's ratings of preacher effectiveness can be predicted by knowing their ratings of "uses natural and effective gestures while preaching." In addition to effective use of gestures, maintaining eye contact and delivering the sermon with enthusiasm appear to be particularly significant nonverbal predictors. The fact that monotone voice, loudness of delivery, and reading the sermon are ranked lower than many other predictors should not obscure the importance of these factors. It is possible that these factors emerged as less important because relatively few preachers in the sample had a problem with monotone voice, loudness, or reading the sermon. The items "lacks enthusiasm," "speaks too much in a monotone voice," and "reads all or most of the sermon" may have been more predictive if they had been phrased in a positive rather than negative manner.

Analyses of Several Predictors Considered Together

A procedure in statistics called "stepwise regression analysis" is capable of determining which subset of a large number of predictors explains the most variability in a "dependent variable" (in our study this is the rating of preacher effectiveness). The prior discussion ranked predictors of preacher effectiveness when considered independently of one another. This section presents the results of stepwise regression analyses that consider the predictors as a group.

The order in which each predictor is listed is significant. The first predictor listed is the one that is most powerful as an individual predictor. The second predictor listed is the variable that explained the most about the remaining variability in preacher ratings that was not explained by the first predictor. The third variable was the one that explained the most about the variability still unexplained by the first two predictors and so on.

It should be noted that stepwise regression analyses are used for exploration of data for which the researcher has few prior hypotheses regarding which variables will be most predictive. The results of these stepwise regressions should be treated as exploratory. Only when much further research has confirmed or refuted the importance of the variables should more firm conclusions be made.

National Sample

When all the predictors from the national sample were considered together, the following three emerged as the most predictive of preacher ratings:

1. This preacher's sermons make me feel like he or she knows what is in my heart.
2. This preacher's style of delivering the sermon helps keep my attention.
3. This preacher's experience of daily life is similar to mine.

Taken together, these three variables were able to explain 91 percent of the variability in preacher ratings.

Catholic Priests Sample

The following six variables were able to account for 85 percent of the variability in ratings of Catholic priests as preachers:

1. This preacher's style of delivering the sermon helps keep my attention.
2. This preacher's sermons make me feel like he or she knows what is in my heart.
3. This preacher helps me get a new or deeper appreciation of the Scripture reading(s).
4. This preacher makes creative use of stories and examples to enhance the sermon.
5. This preacher's sermons are relevant to my daily life.
6. This preacher usually presents ideas in the sermon very similar to my own.

The next fourteen variables to enter the regression analysis were able to explain only an additional 2 percent of variability in ratings of overall preacher effectiveness.

Catholic Deacons Sample

The following six variables were able to explain 76 percent of the variability in ratings of deacons as preachers:

1. The preacher helps me get a new or deeper appreciation of the Scripture reading(s).
2. This preacher's style of delivering the sermon helps keep my attention.
3. This preacher makes creative use of stories or examples to enhance the sermon.
4. This preacher usually presents ideas in the sermon very similar to my own.
5. This preacher uses humor effectively in sermons.
6. This preacher's sermons make me feel like he or she knows what is in my heart.

The next seven predictors could explain only an additional 3 percent of variability.

Workshop Sample

The following four variables were able to explain 76 percent of the variability in ratings of the five preachers in this sample:

1. This preacher's sermons usually have a clear central message.
2. This preacher's sermons make me feel like he or she knows what is in my heart.
3. This preacher's style of delivering the sermon helps keep my attention.
4. This preacher's experience of daily life is similar to mine.

Discussion of Stepwise Regression Analyses

Two predictors emerged in the regression analyses of all four samples: "keeps my attention" and "knows what is in my heart." These data represent a replication of the importance of these two variables across four independent samples of listeners. These two factors emerged as the first two variables to enter the regression analysis in the national and priests samples.

The deacons regression analysis was quite different from the national and priests samples. Most important for deacons appears to be an ability to give the listener a deeper appreciation of Scripture and to maintain attention through creative stories, examples, and humor. "Knowing what is in my heart" was the sixth variable to enter the regression for deacons, indicating that it was less predictive for this group of preachers.

Summary of Findings

Four major findings from the numerical data analyses in this study are summarized below:

1. Listeners' ratings of specific preachers on five ratings variables were highly correlated. While future studies may investigate further specific nuances of listeners' ratings of preachers, *the results of this study indicate that an underlying global evaluation of a preacher is formed in the listener's mind.* It appears that a listener either likes or does not like a preacher's sermons/homilies. The data presented here do not indicate that listeners make finer distinctions in rating preachers.

2. The top ten survey items (in terms of their ability to predict how preachers were rated by listeners), considering the results of the national, priests, and deacons samples were as follows:
   1) keeps my attention
   2) knows what is in my heart
   3) gives me a new or deeper appreciation of Scripture
   4) has a clear central message

      5) is relevant to my daily life
      6) makes creative use of stories and examples
      7) uses humor effectively
      8) presents ideas very similar to my own
      9) is a likable person
      10) knows the real struggles of life

3. Nonverbal elements related to the preacher's delivery of the sermon or homily were correlated with overall preacher ratings. These variables, while not emerging in the top ten predictors, appear to be an important part of how preachers are evaluated by listeners.

4. Regression analyses on all four samples indicated that when several predictors are considered together, they can account for a large percentage of the variability in how preachers are rated.

Two predictors were present in the regression analyses in all four samples: *keeps my attention* and *knows what is in my heart*.

Recommendations and Possibilities for Future Research

The research presented in this appendix represents a small beginning to what could be an exciting new field of research: the empirical study of preaching. This section briefly describes a number of future studies that would increase our knowledge about effective preaching. Physicians use research to improve their treatment of the body, and psychologists use research to improve their efforts with mind and emotions. It is time for preachers to use research to improve the effectiveness of their efforts to speak to the human soul.

The number of studies that could be conducted on preaching is limited only by a researcher's creative imagination. This section will attempt only to give examples of the types of studies that are possible.

Replication

No research finding can be considered solid until it is replicated by other researchers. This is to ensure that biases of one particular researcher do not unknowingly slant the data. While the research presented in this book contained some replication (for instance, results from the national, Catholic priest, Catholic deacon, and workshop samples all indicated that "keeps my attention" is a key determinant of how preachers are rated), further replication by other researchers is necessary to solidify these findings.

Development of Standardized Research Instruments

The survey used for this study was developed specifically for this study. Attempts to replicate the research presented in this book may best be done by using the same survey we used. Over time, however, future research could focus on developing briefer, more user-friendly, psychometrically tested instruments for studying preacher effectiveness.

Many areas of research within the field of psychology are unfortunately unclear because researchers use their own measurement instruments (tests or surveys, for instance). This makes comparing results across studies difficult. It is far better for standardized instruments to be developed that allow for straightforward comparison between studies.

Specific Research Ideas

Future research on preacher effectiveness could address the following questions:

1. What factors lead to long-term retention of preachers' messages? This research could be conducted using a survey similar to the one we used. Alternatively, in-depth interviews with those who listen to preaching could uncover the common aspects of the homilies or sermons that they can remember months or years after they heard them.

2. Is there a correlation between preacher effectiveness and charitable giving to the church? Between preacher effectiveness and attendance at church services?

3. If "keeps my attention" is one of the most important determinants of effective preaching, what factors most effectively lead to maintaining attention: sharing of personal experiences, speaking to human concerns, using humor, sharing relevant stories, delivering with effective nonverbals?

4. What factors in the content or delivery of a sermon lead to the listener feeling the preacher "knows what is in my heart"?

5. Are male and female preachers perceived differently? If so, are they perceived differently by male and female listeners?

6. How is the length of the sermon correlated with ratings of the effectiveness of the sermon? An expected result would be an "inverted U" relationship. Very brief and very long sermons would be expected to be rated as less effective than sermons of moderate length.

7. Does the perception of preaching differ between those who regularly attend church services and those who attend infrequently or not at all?

8. If "here-and-now" (relevant to daily life) sermons are rated as more effective than "there-and-then" (focused on Bible history) or "up there" (too theological, abstract), what is the most effective use of history and theology in a sermon? For instance, these factors could be studied using three videotaped versions of the same sermon—one focused solely on the here and now, one with historical material added, and one with theological material added.

9. If similarity between the preacher's and listeners' ideas is an important determinant of preacher ratings, how can preachers effectively deliver messages that are discrepant from listeners' views?

10. Is there a difference between "listener ratings of preacher effectiveness" and "preacher effectiveness"? In other words, is how well people like a homily or sermon the best measure of its effectiveness? If not, how else can preacher effectiveness be measured?

11. Can it be shown empirically that using ongoing peer or congregational evaluation of a preacher's effectiveness can improve the preacher's effectiveness?

12. In this study, an overall rating variable was used because analysis showed that respondents' answers to five rating items were highly correlated. Further research is needed to explore the following question: Do listeners mainly use a global judgment of preacher effectiveness, or do they make finer distinctions not detected in this study?

13. Is there a place for using negatively worded survey items—perhaps to study ineffective preaching?

14. Are deacons and priests really perceived on average to be equivalent in preaching effectiveness (as the results of this study indicate)? Or were this study's results affected strongly by selection bias (for instance, perhaps only the most confident deacons chose to include themselves in the study)?

The above list of ideas is only a minimal beginning. As research is conducted and published, new questions will emerge from the research and the field of the empirical study of preaching will be on its way. While an empirical approach to preaching may seem strange to some who are used to thinking of religion and science as distinct realms, the results of the data presented in this book indicate that a systematic program of studying preaching empirically could greatly enhance our understanding of this important activity. With greater understanding should come the ability to train preachers to carry out more effectively the vital task of preaching.

Suggested Resources

Books on the Preacher's Craft

Bond, D. Stephenson. *Interactive Preaching*. St. Louis: CBP Press, 1991.

Burghardt, Walter J. *Preaching: The Art and the Craft*. New York: Paulist Press, 1987.

Buttrick, David. *Homiletic: Moves and Structures*. Philadelphia: Fortress Press, 1987.

Craddock, Fred B. *Preaching*. Nashville: Abingdon, 1985.

Hilkert, Mary Catherine. *Naming Grace: Preaching and the Sacramental Imagination*. New York: Continuum, 1997.

Long, Thomas G. *The Witness of Preaching*. Louisville: Westminster John Knox, 1989.

Scott, John. *Between Two Worlds*. Grand Rapids: Eerdmans, 1982.

Untener, Ken. *Preaching Better: Practical Suggestions for Homilists*. New York: Paulist Press, 1999.

Books on Theology and Scripture

Balthasar, Hans Urs von. *Light of the Word: Brief Reflections on the Sunday Readings*. San Francisco: Ignatius Press, 1993.

Barth, Karl. *Dogmatics in Outline*. New York: Harper, 1959.

Brown, Raymond E. *An Introduction to the New Testament*. Anchor Bible Reference Library. New York: Doubleday, 1997.

Küng, Hans. *On Being a Christian*. Translated by Edward Quinn, Garden City, NY: Image, 1984.

Macquarrie, John. *Principles of Christian Theology*. London: SCM Press, 2003.

Rahner, Karl. *Foundations of Christian Faith: An Introduction to the Idea of Christianity*. New York: Crossroad, 1982.

————. *The Great Church Year.* New York: Crossroad, 1993.

Tillich, Paul. *The New Being.* Introduction by Mary Ann Stenger. Lincoln: University of Nebraska Press, 2005.

————. *Systematic Theology.* Chicago: University of Chicago Press, 1967.

Periodicals

America, Christian Century, Christianity Today, and *Commonweal* are among the periodicals that help preachers keep up-to-date. *Interpretation* (Union Theological Seminary, Richmond, Virginia) has a regular feature on preaching. *New Theology Review* (Catholic Theological Union of Chicago and Washington) provides a similar service.

Biblical Commentaries

Brown, Raymond E., et al., eds. *The New Jerome Biblical Commentary.* Englewood Cliffs, NJ: Prentice-Hall, 1989.

Freedman, David Noel, ed. *The Anchor Bible Dictionary.* 6 vols. New York: Doubleday, 1992.

The following are lectionary-based commentaries:

Bergant, Dianne, with Richard Fragomeni. *Preaching the New Lectionary.* Collegeville, MN: Liturgical Press, 1999–2001.

Craddock, Fred B., et al., *Preaching through the Christian Year: A Comprehensive Commentary on the Lectionary.* Valley Forge, PA: Trinity Press International, 1992–94.

Faley, Roland J. *Footprints on the Mountain: Preaching and Teaching the Sunday Readings.* New York: Paulist Press, 1994.

Fuller, Reginald. *Preaching the Lectionary: The Word of God for the Church Today.* Rev. ed. Collegeville, MN: Liturgical Press, 1984.

Biblical Dictionary

Stuhlmueller, Carroll, et al., eds. *The Collegeville Pastoral Dictionary of Biblical Theology.* Collegeville, MN: Liturgical Press, 1996.